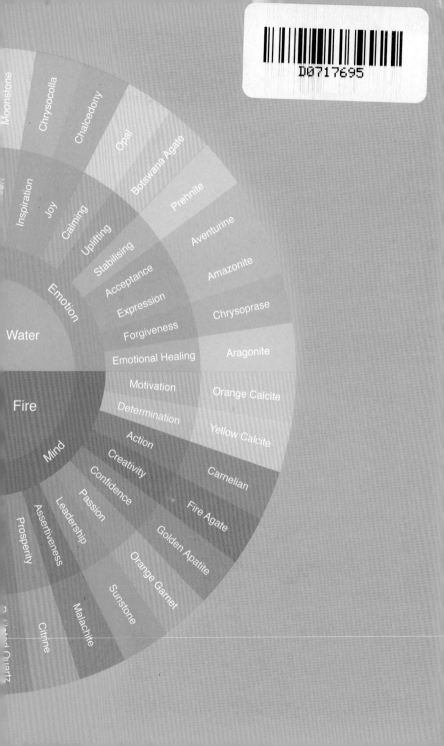

Moonstone

Chrysocolla

Chalcedony

Opal

Botswana Agate

Prehnite

Inspiration

Joy

Calming

Uplifting

Aventurine

Stabilising

Acceptance

Amazonite

Emotion

Expression

Chrysoprase

Water

Forgiveness

Aragonite

Emotional Healing

Motivation

Orange Calcite

Fire

Determination

Yellow Calcite

Action

Mind

Creativity

Confidence

Carnelian

Passion

Leadership

Fire Agate

Assertiveness

Golden Apatite

Prosperity

Orange Garnet

Sunstone

Malachite

Citrine

# THE
# CRYSTAL
# COMPASS

# THE CRYSTAL COMPASS

A guide to using crystals for energy, healing
& reclaiming your power

AISHA AMARFIO

First published in Great Britain in 2018 by Orion Spring
an imprint of The Orion Publishing Group Ltd
Carmelite House, 50 Victoria Embankment
London EC4Y 0DZ
An Hachette UK Company
1 3 5 7 9 10 8 6 4 2

ISBN: 978 1 4091 7694 7

Printed in Great Britain by CPI Group (UK) Ltd, Croydon, CR0 4YY

MIX
Paper from
responsible sources
FSC® C104740

www.orionbooks.co.uk

ORION
SPRING

# Contents

Foreword                                                    1

Introduction                                                3

**1  Energy Healing**                                      **23**

**2  Identifying the Root of our Energy Imbalances  41**

**3  Using Crystals**                                     **53**

**4  Earth**                                              **71**

Pyrite                    Energising                       82
Hematite                  Grounding                        85
Mookaite (Mook Jasper)    Rejuvenation                     88
Jade                      Health                           90
Obsidian                  Protection                       93
Onyx                      Strength                         97
Smoky Quartz              Relaxing                         99
Tiger's Eye               Security and Stability          101
Black Tourmaline          Purification                    104
Bloodstone                Courage                         107

**5 Water** **111**

| | | |
|---|---|---|
| Moonstone | Intuition | 130 |
| Chrysocolla | Inspiration | 134 |
| Chalcedony | Joy | 137 |
| Opal (Common) | Calming | 140 |
| Botswana Agate | Uplifting | 143 |
| Prehnite | Stabilising | 145 |
| Aventurine | Acceptance | 147 |
| Amazonite | Expression | 150 |
| Chrysoprase | Forgiveness | 153 |
| Aragonite (Blue) | Emotional Healing | 156 |

**6 Fire** **159**

| | | |
|---|---|---|
| Orange Calcite | Motivation | 172 |
| Yellow Calcite | Determination | 174 |
| Carnelian | Action | 176 |
| Fire Agate | Creativity | 179 |
| Golden (Yellow) Apatite | Confidence | 181 |
| Orange (Spessartite) Garnet | Passion | 184 |
| Sunstone | Leadership | 187 |
| Malachite | Assertiveness | 189 |
| Citrine | Prosperity | 192 |
| Rutilated Quartz | Decisiveness | 194 |

## 7  Air                                                    197

| Rose Quartz | Love | 210 |
|---|---|---|
| Labradorite | Magic | 212 |
| Purple Fluorite | Psychic Clarity | 215 |
| Amethyst | Spiritual Healing | 218 |
| Apophyllite | Spiritual Awareness | 220 |
| Lapis Lazuli | Self-knowledge | 222 |
| Selenite | Faith | 224 |
| Sodalite | Insight | 226 |
| Optical Calcite | Divine Purpose | 229 |
| Blue Lace Agate | Communication | 232 |

## 8  The Cure-All                                           235

| Conclusion | 237 |
|---|---|
| Symptoms Index | 241 |
| Results Index | 243 |
| Acknowledgements | 245 |
| About the Author | 247 |

# Foreword

Crystals are little pieces of earth, love and magic. We all need a little magic injected in our lives. With the unending demands of daily life, the unhealthy pressures from social conditioning and the endless chatter in our heads, we can become lost and forgetful of who we are; we can become disconnected from our depths and start to wonder what life is all about.

Often feelings of being lost, anxious, exhausted or low are a longing for us to go within; a longing for us discover our true self; a longing for us to find deeper meaning, purpose and connection.

Crystals can help us respond to that call. Crystals, like everything in the universe, are alive with spirit. The more we are connected with the spirit of life, the more we are connected with our soul and the magic and miraculous energy that links us all.

Crystals give us a safe space to check in with the more soulful parts of who we are. They help us to amplify our wisdom and harness the power of our intuition, so that we can listen to our bodies, work with rather than against our emotions, reclaim our power and express our soul dream.

*The Crystal Compass* offers a companion on your spiritual healing journey, using crystals to reconnect with your truth, the universe and who you are in your soul. It covers 40 of the most abundant and practical crystals, across the elements of Earth, Water, Fire and Air, with each element representing key areas in life.

Through energy healing exercises and a catalogue of crystal properties for each element, *The Crystal Compass* seeks to become a tool to help you find balance, express your gifts and navigate your soul path.

# Introduction

## MY STORY

I clearly remember my first interaction with crystals. My mum and I were walking on our way somewhere, and I noticed a crystal shop nearby. I knew absolutely nothing about crystals, but I felt so compelled to go in. Crystals have a way of having that effect on people. They call you.

I was called. The rest is history.

From the moment we walked in, I was hooked. It felt like I was home. I was immediately in love with all these little magic beings from the earth. They held a purity of life force that for those short moments shifted me to a peaceful state; beyond the pressures of daily life outside. The crystals spoke to me, and though I had no conscious idea of what they were saying, I could just feel their sense of cosmic harmony being transmitted right through me, and in my excitement, intrigue and curiosity, I was desperate to know more.

I gravitated towards specific crystals and bought a purple fluorite, whose structure and colour fascinated me. That was ten years ago. As I sit here and write this, that purple fluorite still sits on my desk today, helping me organise my thoughts.

On reflection, I can honestly say that entering that shop was my entry into my own spiritual healing journey. Crystals introduced me to deeper dimensions of who I am and became tools of support in everything I did. A bit overexcitedly at first, I admit. I had them under my pillow to help me understand my dreams, tucked in my pockets to give me confidence, stuffed in my bag to promote prosperity and protection; I had so many crystals in my room it was becoming a bit of a cave.

I would count down the hours at work in my eagerness to get home to just sit and meditate with my crystals like a hermit; and if I was staying the night anywhere I would take a shedload of crystals with me, just in case. Just in case of what, I don't know. It was all bit obsessive, and crossing the line into unnecessary nerdy behaviour territory, but it was a sign. Because when you want to live and breathe something, you know you are on to a passion on your soul path.

Looking back, I can chart how crystals cleared me of many blockages and gave me incredible experiences that taught me about the nature of energy. From kundalini experiences to orgasmic heart awakenings, crystals taught me, by initiation, about the fundamental role that energy plays in every layer of our being.

I studied crystals with several crystal healers and immersed myself in books, but my greatest time was spent just learning from the crystals themselves. Because they are the best teachers. Crystals became my allies, and helped guide me through the fears, through the lack of confidence, through the negative beliefs and the difficult experiences. They helped me to reveal my strength, listen to my intuition and make life choices that were true to my soul.

Today, I am an energy healer and use crystals in my practice to help others on their path. I spent six years in training and initiation to become a reiki master and a shamanic energy healer.

Reiki healing is a means of channelling universal life force energy through your hands on to a recipient to bring about balance. Shamanism is an ancient practice that attends to the healing needs of our soul, which is so often missing in our modern-day hustle and bustle. Shamanism involves deep relationship and communion with spirit and nature to access the harmonic wisdom of the whole. Shamanic energy healing is about awakening people's soul gifts and their innate capacity for healing, growth and transformation; it seeks to get to the energetic root cause of an issue or a life pattern that a person is facing, by removing energetic blockages and restoring their energy to be in harmony with their soul.

Becoming a shamanic healer and reiki master helped me to deepen my practice of energy work with crystals. Working with crystals over the years, I discovered that crystals are little shamanic healers and reiki masters themselves. They are master channels of life force energy, each with their own unique quality. And just like a shaman, they tune you into yourself and the rest of the universe so that you can unlock your deepest wisdom, reclaim your power and reconnect with your soul to be the fullest version of you.

In this book I combine my experience of shamanism and energy healing with my knowledge of crystals to offer a healing journey where you can reconnect with your soul, using crystals as your personal on-hand shamanic energy healers.

There are common misconceptions about what shamanism is. To me, shamanism is our most ancient and natural way to tune in to the spirit and oneness of life, to come into wholeness and soulful relationship with the world. It is a way to work in harmony with life force energy, which is in tune to the whole, and is always guiding us on our path.

Tuning in often means us finding a quiet moment where we can soften the chatter and attachments of our conscious minds, and bring our awareness to the signs and signals of the soul's dream that is being communicated through us all the time, through our body, our emotions, our mind and our spiritual awareness of the universe.

Some of our oldest practices for tuning in are meditation, prayer, inner work, yoga and the shamanic journey. The shamanic journey is a method of expanding our awareness, to include both the physical reality and the spiritual reality that exists behind it. Shamanic journeying often utilises rhythms of drumming or rattling, to shift us into a state of consciousness where we can be more in tune with the spiritual nature of life.

In a shamanic journey, you can seek the guidance of your soul's dream and the guidance of all the unified field's dreamers, entering a spiritual space, where you can perceive the wisdom of your true self and the multiple expression of life's guides and allies that are pointing you in the right direction all the time. Shamanic journeying is an entry to the rich landscape of the psyche and its expansive gateway to the spiritual reality that is the oneness of life.

It might sound all very mystical, but it is the most natural and primal human ability and relationship, and we unconsciously do it all the time in our dreaming or in moments when we are feeling very intuitive – we are just tapping into a spiritual landscape. It all starts with our trust, faith and our conscious intention to tune in.

One evening, I was feeling really lost and restless about life so I took my tension into a shamanic journey to seek guidance as to what it was about. Why do I feel this way? What should I do? In the journey I received the soul dream guidance that 'It is time to write a book.' I had played with this idea before, but I never had the confidence or belief that it was really possible and I was unclear about how it would work for me. How would I start? How would I get it published? Am I qualified enough to speak? I'm not good at writing, it'll be too hard. These were the energy blockages of old insecurities that my soul dream's communication was trying to fight through, causing tension. But still the guidance reached me and was clear, that it was time for me to write a book.

So I accepted the guidance, discarded the seeds of doubt and made an inner decision to boldly explore making that happen somehow, some way. But I didn't have to. A few days after receiving the guidance of that shamanic journey, I received an email out of the blue from Orion publishers, asking me in for a meeting to discuss the possibility of writing a book about crystals and healing ... Ta-da!! With the power of my inner decision aligned to my soul and trusting the flow, my soul dream had triumphed in bringing itself forth through the magic and interconnectivity of life.

Life is always asking us to hear the wisdom of our soul dream wherever we face an inner conflict. The experience of inner conflict, if unheard or unresolved, may even cause a physical, emotional, mental or spiritual tension that will only worsen when we side with our own resistance to the change that our soul dream is asking for; whether it is to change an attitude, to move out of a relationship, to forgive someone or to change a job, or to make any life decision that will better serve our truth. In the symptoms of tension, there are always emergent messages of soul guidance trying to come through, acting in opposition to our unconscious fear-based reasoning that thinks it knows best. The wisdom of the soul lies in all symptoms of tension; we just have to learn how to listen to it. The more we get to know ourselves and the way in which our soul dream communicates through our tension, the clearer our soul dream guidance becomes. But that can be tricky; sometimes we can feel really low, or lost or riddled with tension, and have no idea of the conflicting energies behind why we feel the way we do; we just have the feeling that something is not quite right with the way we are living life.

The shamanic journey, or any form of spiritual practice of bringing our conscious awareness to the spiritual nature of what is going on in our lives, is a more deliberate and intentional means of accessing soul dream guidance in our tension. It requires us to release our attachment to any stance or mood we are occupying, so that we can allow whatever it is that needs to come up, to come up. When we create a sacred, spiritual and quiet space to check in with ourselves, and give our conscious awareness to what is coming up in our tension, we can often become clear what change is being asked of us in our life.

On this rare occasion in my shamanic journey where I was told it was time to write a book, the soul dream guidance was crystal clear (excuse the pun), which was great! But it can often take me way more effort to decipher the guidance than that; sometimes I don't hear the wisdom in my tension and I get stuck in limiting patterns, until I do. It's not always simple, but it's all part of the process and beautiful journey towards discovering our truth. The more sacred space we create in our lives to check in with our symptoms of tension and what is trying to be expressed, the more we can deepen our intuition and listen to our soul; and the more we do that, the easier and more magical the journey becomes.

Crystals give us that sacred space; healing exercises and meditation with crystals, or even just wearing crystals, creates space, stillness and intentionality in our lives for us to unlock our wisdom and our soul gifts within. Crystals amplify parts of the soul's dream that are seeking to come through in our lives, and they ease the conditioned or chaotic parts of us that may be blocking that. The soul dream will always bring through a quality you need to express in your life to be the fullest version of you. In our anxiety, courage is waiting to come through, in our weakness, strength is waiting to come through, in our darkest hour, our light is waiting to lift us. Sometimes we have to know the polarities of what we are not, to discover the fullness of what we are. Through amplifying the more soulful parts of ourselves, crystals help us to heal, overcome obstacles and become more whole.

## THE SOUL DREAM AND HEALING

We live in a dreaming universe and you are an expression of your soul's dreaming within it. Your soul dream is your reason for being; that which gives you meaning; that which wants to be expressed and come into fruition in the world, as a unique service to the whole.

Like the acorn holds the dream of an age-old oak tree, your soul dream is the seed of potentiality of who you really are, in your highest expression. Whereas the realisation of the oak tree's soul dream is hardwired in its biology and brought into being by natural and divine forces, we have to *consciously* discover and nurture our soul dream to realise its highest expression. You nurture the seed of your soul dream and bring it into realisation with the Earth of your body, the Water of your emotions and intuition, the Fire of your mind and power of will, and the Air of your spirit and its connection to the divine.

Do you remember your soul dream?
Do you remember why you came here?
Do you nurture your seed?

The soul dream isn't a desire of your ego, or something to work towards or a goal to achieve; it is rather a fluid and authentic expression of your soul's truth and gifts, and its deeper connection to the oneness of all there is. Healing is the journey towards balance and wholeness. In healing, we often think that our physical, emotional or mental symptoms of tension are the thing that is wrong with us, the thing that we need to fix or get rid of to become whole. But what if we instead treated our symptoms of tension as signals from the soul's dreaming; signals that are trying to tell us something; signals that are indicating that a change is being asked of us from within to reconnect with our truth.

Our soul's intelligence acts in a compensatory nature. If we are being too one-sided in our approach to life and are too attached to beliefs, desires or ideals that are not true to our soul, the soul's intelligence will compensate by trying to push through a different soul quality to counteract our one-sidedness. The conflicting energy between these two parts of ourselves, our conditioned self and our soul, is what we experience as tension or inner conflict. The tension is only the signal indicating that something is suppressing our connection to our soul and the expression of its dream.

The more we resist or ignore the signal and the direction of change our soul is asking for, the louder the signal will get, until it, at worst, becomes unbearable. For example, I used to suffer with terrible anxiety and panic attacks. I would treat the anxiety as the problem. I would treat it as something that was 'wrong' with me. A sickness and an unreasonable response to the world that I needed to 'manage' or 'cope with'. But life isn't for managing or coping. Life is for living fully and fluidly, with

—
11

everything that comes up. I asked myself, what if my anxiety *is* a reasonable response to something, what if my anxiety is a sensation indicating something deeper within? Anxiety may not look neat or rational, or conform to how society has conditioned me to be accepted as normal and productive in the world, but what if I threw that away for a moment and enquired with my soul what the root of the anxiety was?

The moment I stopped treating my anxiety as the problem, and started listening to what my anxiety was asking of me, my life changed.

I noticed the energy behind all the situations that my anxiety was triggered in. The anxiety arose when I was operating from an energy of 'I am not enough, so I have to try and do more'. I wasn't aware that this was the energy and belief behind all my experiences. It was such an old and deep-rooted unconscious belief that it was an autopilot mode which had just become so normal for me. I simply wasn't aware that that was the energy going on in the background of all my behaviours and actions. This belief was embedded so deep in my psyche, a wound in my ego from my past, but it was very present, as it was the space where all my actions came from. It gave rise to a pattern of behaviour where I would always strive for perfection or overcompensate by over-extending myself for others, in order to gain approval while doing a million and one things in my work life to prove I am enough.

You can get a sense of how depleting this is! When you are coming from an energy of lack or deficit, and then from this space you are expending huge amounts of energy, exerting yourself outwardly to 'prove' yourself, it's like trying to drive a car really fast with an empty tank. You will eventually become energetically depleted, and at worst crash out. I did, by the way, crash out several times, until I eventually got the point.

What we manifest is reflective of the energy we are coming from. Energy medicine is discerning the energy behind things. What is the energy behind your thoughts, feelings, emotions or behaviours? Is it an energy of wholeness or deficit?

The scale of wholeness, peace and fulfilment we experience is a direct measure of the space or energy we are coming from. When we are coming from a space of integrated wholeness rather than lack or deficit or conflict, we are operating on a full tank, in flow with life force; that which is infinite and our truth. From this space we have nothing to prove. We are working in service to our soul's dreaming, and can be energetically lifted and nourished and feel purposeful and fulfilled by whatever we are doing.

In my times of anxiety, I called on crystals simply to help me ease the symptoms, because we all know how uncomfortable anxiety can be. I just wanted it to go away so I could be normal and get on with my ego's fantasies of what I thought life should be like. I got more than I bargained for. Instead of just relieving the anxiety, crystals helped me unlock the soul wisdom beneath it to show me what my anxiety was asking of me. Change.

Crystals helped reveal the unconscious conditioned beliefs of my ego's dreams that were in the way of my soul's. They helped me identify the beliefs about not being enough and let them go, so that I could reclaim my power and move in a new direction. Your unconscious conditioned beliefs just want you to get on with life the way you're living it. Your soul wants you to expand into the whole, which means moving in a new direction, the direction of your soul dream.

So my anxiety wasn't the problem – the anxiety was just the sensation of tension between the old unconscious beliefs that were operating in *resistance* to the emergent qualities of my soul. Once I revealed the energy of the unconscious beliefs, I could reclaim my power from them and follow the pull of the soul dream.

Crystals aren't just about relieving symptoms or manifesting our ego's desires. Many practices show us how to numb or fix the symptoms because they think the symptoms are the problem, because they are so uncomfortable. But that is not true healing, true healing is about revealing the wisdom beneath the symptoms so that you can experience the life change your soul wants. If you try to numb, suppress, ignore or fix the symptom, the symptom won't go away, it'll just become more pronounced or it will find another channel to express itself through.

Behind my anxiety, my unconscious belief of 'I am not enough, I have to try and do more' was operating in conflict with my soul's core wisdom that 'I am' is enough. And every time I was unconsciously acting from that conflicted place, anxiety would flare up to show me that.

I finally listened to what my soul's wisdom was telling me through my symptoms. And if I hadn't listened, I probably would have been crippled by my anxiety. My overextending was taking me in the wrong direction, in my work life, in my relationships and in my health.

In the conflict and chaos of our unconscious beliefs and our blocked energy, crystals amplify the wholeness of our soul, so that we can find the path of least resistance to self-knowledge, enlightenment and the expression of our soul's dreaming.

To help us in our work with crystals it can be useful to ask ourselves the right questions. Self-knowledge comes from being clear about the energy we are coming from and how our soul communicates through us. Some helpful questions are:

- What is the energy behind how I am feeling? What I am thinking? What I am doing?
- Am I being true to myself?
- What space am I operating from, wholeness or deficit, lack and conflict?
- Is this relationship or pattern energetically depleting me or nourishing me?
- Am I working towards or away from my soul's dream?
- What soul quality in me is trying to be expressed?

By bringing our conscious awareness to our blockage or symptom with self-enquiry, we can:

know how our unconscious beliefs come up in our feelings, thought patterns and behaviours.

know when we are being true to our soul by seeing whether or not our behaviour is congruent with our soul's dream.

know whether we are creating a life of lack and deficit or wholeness.

know which relationships are serving us and which are not.

know which decisions are going to nourish the seed of our soul dream into full fruition in the physical world.

And the joy about all of this is that we have everything we need to do it.

We have been given this beautiful navigation system of the Earth of our body, the Water of our emotions, our feelings and our intuition, and the Fire of our intellect and mind to help us discern whether we are on track or not.

We just have to unify these faculties with the Air of our spirit so that we can be in alignment with our spiritual path and potential.

When it becomes a little too chaotic, conflicted and stormy inside and we need to find our unifying centre of stillness to remind us of how we can harness the power of our navigation system, crystals can give us that stillness. And when we need a little help to understand ourselves better and need a little strength or any other quality we might be lacking in order to make that change, crystals can unlock that strength.

## THE HISTORY OF CRYSTALS AND THEIR POWERS

Crystals have always been venerated and have been a consistent feature in our experience of the mystical and divine. Humans across cultures and time have been intuitively drawn to using crystals for healing, divination, good fortune, power, protection and beauty.

Whether used as jewels for symbols of power in regal or priestly headwear, or used in healing ceremonies by our ancestors, or in components in the hardware of our technology that we use every day, crystals have played a role in human history, culture and science as precious objects that conduct energy for transformative and magical uses. They have even been misused for their powers. We don't have to look far in our folklore to find stories of stones with special powers being abused or myths of cursed gems bringing misfortune to their owners. These themes are still prevalent on our screens and in literature today.

The practice of using crystals for metaphysical purposes can be traced back across the ancient worlds. The crystal ball has been a tool for fortune-telling since Greek and Roman times, and crystals have been used for healing and seeing into the future in the ancient traditions of the Druids, the Incas, the Egyptians, the Dagara, the Persians, the Chinese, the Mayans and the many native tribes of North America. In the more recent history of eighteenth-century Europe, the practice of associating crystals with months of the year gave rise to the widespread custom of wearing birthstone jewellery for good luck and prosperity, which is still popular across the world today.

Today crystals are being recognised more and more for their properties and healing ability and have become widely used by many.

## HOW CRYSTALS WORK

Crystals are channels of life force energy and have a correcting effect on our energy field, according to our needs and the properties of the crystal. They act as conductors, amplifiers and purifiers that transmit and transform our energy in line with their unique set of qualities. They can clear us of energies that no longer serve us and realign our energy to be in harmony with our soul, to restore wellbeing, vitality and the expression of our higher gifts.

Using crystals is not about forcing what we are not, it is about working with life force to bring through what we are.

Crystals are perfect structures of wholeness, harmony and balance, created by the magic of nature's forces.

Millions of years ago, the elements of Earth, Water, Fire and Air collided in the crevices and caves of the earth's layers. Gas, pressure, heat, moisture and cooling combined with the minerals of the earth, and over periods of thousands of years, these elemental dynamics brought about the formation of crystals; highly ordered lattice structures of different geometric shapes, colours and sizes.

Crystals not only contain an extraordinarily high level of order in their structure, they hold a resonance of the earth's magnetic field, and are pulsating with the qualities of the elements that combined and formed them deep within the earth. This high level of order and harmony imbued with the qualities of the elements is what gives crystals their healing properties. They are energy conductors and have the power to transform frequencies of dissonance and chaos into frequencies of harmony and order.

The elements of Earth, Water, Fire and Air are primal aspects of all of the physical universe, and each element represents a set of metaphysical qualities that relate to an aspect of our life and an area of our health, wellbeing and personal development.

## ELEMENTAL QUALITIES FOR WHOLENESS

**Earth** is the foundation of matter; inwardly, it represents the body and our health. Outwardly, Earth signifies us manifesting strong foundations in our home life, careers and in the immediate network and ecosystem that we can call our surrounding support and community.

**Water** is our sensory experience of life; inwardly, it signifies our ability to process the wisdom of our emotions and our intuition. Outwardly, our water element relates to healthy functioning of intimate relationships with our self and others.

**Fire** is the direction of will, power and transformation; inwardly, it relates to our mental energy and outwardly it signifies our ability to exert our mind and consciously direct our power towards manifesting ourselves in the world.

**Air** is the space and spiritual oneness that hosts all the elements. Inwardly and outwardly it relates to the light of our awareness that has the power to bring consciousness to our truth and unify our connection within the whole.

Crystals contain a harmonic synthesis of all the elements so they are holistic, but each crystal family has a predominant element, which gives it its quality.

When we are facing an imbalance in a quality of one of the elements, we can turn to crystals for help. *The Crystal Compass* organises 40 crystals by their element and quality, to form a compass that can help you navigate your soul path in all areas of your life and personal development.

For each element, there is a chapter taking you through a holistic healing journey, where you can identify any energy imbalances in that area of your life, and choose a corresponding crystal to work with that will help you to reclaim your vitality and your soul dream guidance.

Each chapter contains a detailed description of the energy body that that element corresponds to, with common symptoms of imbalances, a toolkit of practical healing exercises that you can perform with the crystals and a catalogue of crystals and their properties.

The Compass itself (see the opposite page), provides a quick reference guide that helps you to easily pick the right crystal at the right time. The Compass breaks down the soul qualities for each element, and the crystal that you can use to bring that quality forth in your life.

Through a journey of the elements and the inner self, crystals of the Compass can help us to:

**Earth** (body): Nourish our body and establish firm foundations in this world.

**Water** (emotion): Work with rather than against our emotions, to unlock our emotional wisdom and intuitive power.

**Fire** (mind/will): Reclaim our power and will, and manifest our soul dream.

**Air** (spirit): Find peace, deep meaning, soulful purpose and connection with all that is.

# THE CRYSTAL COMPASS

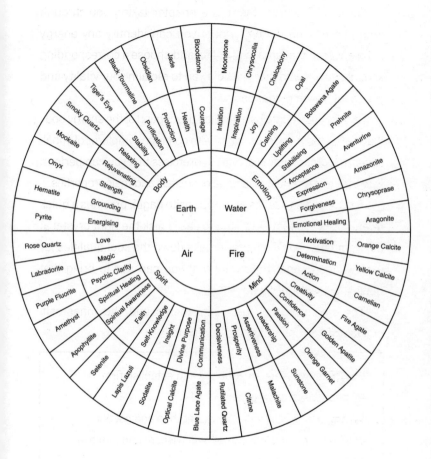

# 1

# Energy Healing

## RECLAIMING OUR CONNECTION

We can encounter energy blockages or lose our energy to all kinds of factors. The overall goal in energy healing is to restore and maintain our energy so that we can consciously align it to our soul and become whole. When we restore and align our energy with our soul and life force, we are at our most vital. When our energy is scattered, blocked or chaotic, we encounter imbalances.

The process of energy healing with crystals in this book is through:

- Reclaiming our lost energy and power
- Clearing ourselves of blockages that are suppressing the soul dream
- Restoring our vitality and connection to our soul and to the divinity of the whole

Being conscious about our vitality requires us to nurture our energy and to protect our energy from relationships with people, environments, jobs, situations, addictions or habits where the energy of the relationship may be oppressive, toxic, or just generally incongruent to the emergent qualities of our soul. If our soul qualities are suppressed in a relationship, and the relationship depletes us of energy, it is time for us to assess the relationship. This is not necessarily an exercise to start blaming relationships or judging the things you have relationships with as bad; it is an exercise about discerning the subjective nature of your relationship, and the energy behind the role you are playing in the relationship, to see whether this role is nourishing to your soul dream or not. That might mean refining the energetic nature of your relationship; it might mean healing the old attachments you have to your role or taking responsibility to heal the wounded part of you that is causing you the most pain or toxicity in the relationship and sometimes it just means cutting an energy dynamic out of your life, and moving on.

This isn't about being egotistical or selfish; it's about being congruent to your truth.

The soul's dreaming is connected to the spiritual nature of reality and the grander web and oneness of life. That which serves the soul, serves the whole. If something isn't serving us, it is probably only serving an old expectation, habit or wounded part of our ego that is seeking some fear-based goal, and isn't really serving anybody in a healthy way.

The approach of energy healing with crystals in this book is based on the principles of honouring and listening to the intelligence of our soul's dreaming as it communicates through the subtle intelligence of our body and our intuition; reclaiming our energy through inner work; and healing relationships in the world where we are losing ourselves and our energy, transmuting goal-based relationships to soul-based ones.

There are crystal meditations for reclaiming our energy and for clearing blockages, and energy audit exercises to assess the energetic quality of the relationships in our lives whether it be to do with work, with people, with habits or with yourself.

Everything is in a relationship with something else. Relationships are the movement and exchange of energy, and the quality of a relationship is determined by the energy behind it. Where there is tension in a relationship, there is an opportunity for healing and resolution in our hearts.

The exercises seek to restore the integrity of our energy, so that we can align it to serve the truth of our soul and give birth to the highest expression of who we really are. Our heart will always tell us if we are there or not and the universe will respond with coincidences that affirm our connection to the oneness and magic of life.

## LIFE FORCE AND ENERGY HEALING

We are beings of life force energy. Life force is the vital force that pervades all living things; it is the self-governing intelligence that powers all of existence. The whole universe is alive with its pulsating force. It is what brings us into being and is an essence that connects us all.

Life force energy perpetuates life, moving it to evolve towards the harmony of the whole. Life force is self-correcting by nature and, through the play of the opposites, it acts in a compensatory nature to bring about states of harmony and balance in life.

We only have to marvel at the self-regulating ecosystem of the rainforest, or the chance movements of the cosmos that bring us life on earth, to see life force's governing impulse towards finding divine equilibrium through chaos.

Life force's balancing nature towards all things being in a state of wholeness is what moves our soul's dreaming; it is what flows through us, giving us health, and vitality and connection to the divine. Our vitality from life force and its connection to the divine is evenly distributed through our physical, emotional, mental and spiritual energy bodies. Each energy body is a gateway to life force and the soul's dreaming, and is a vital part of our conscious experience, providing an interface through which we express and experience the intelligence and individuality of our soul.

When we are aligned, present and in flow with life force, we can be receptive to its self-correcting nature in our lives and follow its path of least resistance towards balance and harmony, working in unison with the rest of life.

Energy imbalances in the energy bodies can block us from this healing quality of life force; manifesting in persistent life patterns, or signs and symptoms that we experience as physical, emotional, mental or spiritual tension.

Holistic energy healing involves us protecting and nourishing the vitality of our energy bodies and listening to them when there is tension, so that we can unlock the wisdom and get to the underlying energy imbalance that it is pointing to. Part of the journey is to heal our blockages and reclaim our energy, power and connection to our soul. Energy healing is a conscious path of self-discovery and realignment with the truth of who we are.

And by being true to ourselves, we can act in service, not because we are trying to be of service, but because when you make a decision that is true to your soul you are acting in the natural vein of life force, which by virtue serves the whole.

Crystals are perfect manifestations of wholeness and can therefore channel the self-correcting nature of life force energy for us, helping us to give vitality to the more soulful parts of us that life is commanding us to bring through, so that we can be the fullest version of ourselves. With our conscious participation, crystals can clear our energy field and help us to address the energy imbalance that is the root cause of an issue in our lives.

## CAUSES OF ENERGY IMBALANCES: WHERE WE LOSE OUR ENERGY

The physical, emotional, mental and spiritual energy bodies each have a role to play in our journey towards finding our truth. They are bodies of intelligence and provide a framework for our soul to experience life and transmit its unique qualities through. When there is an imbalance in our energy body, it disrupts our vitality and compromises our relationship to our soul, resulting in a tension in the way we feel inside, or at worst a physical illness.

As we know, the two main types of imbalances are an energy blockage, or an energy loss in an energy body.

When an energy body has an imbalance it falls out of alignment with our soul and that dissonance is emitted in our energy field.

Energy blockages are stagnant or toxic energies that are

incongruent to our truth and wellbeing; they tend to block emergent parts of our soul that are seeking to be expressed in our life. Common sources of energy blockages are mainly our own unconscious beliefs that we have been conditioned with, that do not match the integrity of the soul dream. Or energy blockages can come from toxic relationships or other people's stuff, that they have projected on to us or that we have just picked up from society or our environments.

Energy loss is when we lose parts of our energy body through shock, trauma, neglect or unhealthy relationship dynamics. Energy loss depletes our vitality levels and has a massive impact on how whole and connected we feel. It also makes us more vulnerable to picking up toxic energy from our surroundings.

Energy is everything. Whatever is going on for us in our energy bodies is transmitted into our energy field. Whatever we emit is the energy that we put out there in the universe. We are transmitting energy signals all the time and our energy field is our energetic language with the rest of the world. The quality of what is happening in our energy field is not only a strong determinant for how we feel, it is a strong determinant for the patterns in our life. Our energy field provides a lens through which we simultaneously perceive and construct our world. The energy we are coming from when we make decisions is the single biggest influencing factor for the energy we invite into our life.

Holistic healing gives us the space and opportunity to listen to our energy bodies and be kind to ourselves; it helps us to take care of our own energy, and be conscious about the energy we bring into our lives.

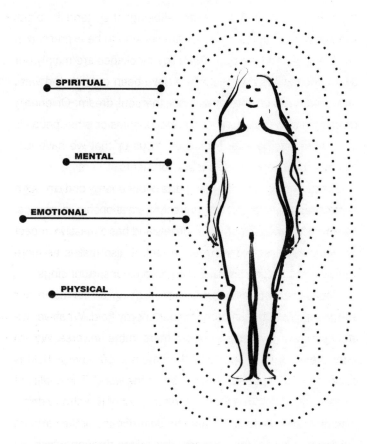

**The above image illustrates the layers of our energy field. The vitality of our energy body is what is transmitted in our energy field. Crystals work by correcting the frequencies in our energy field to harmonise the imbalance in our energy body.**

# COMMON SOURCES OF ENERGY IMBALANCES

## THE VITALITY OF OUR PHYSICAL ENERGY BODY

The physical layer is the first layer of our energy field and pertains to our Earth element. It is responsible for bringing in life force from the universe to give our bodies the vitality we need to house the soul. This layer of our energy field transmits the all-round health of our physical bodies. Energy blockages in this layer occur in our instinctual realms and include deep-rooted family or ancestral patterns or beliefs about money, health or survival. Common sources of energy loss are physical neglect, harm, lack of security and stability or not meeting the body's basic needs for food, water, exercise, rest, breathing and access to nature. Energy imbalances in this area can result in stress, poor health and exhaustion, and patterns of not being able to manifest firm home and financial conditions for ourselves.

## THE VITALITY OF OUR EMOTIONAL ENERGY BODY

The emotional layer is the second layer of our energy field and pertains to our Water element. The emotional energy body is responsible for feeling and intuiting our way through life experiences so that we can grow, mature and change from them. This layer of our energy body transmits the frequencies of our emotions, our sensory experiences and our sexual energy. Common sources of energy blockages that are transmitted in this layer are conflicting or chaotic frequencies of unresolved or suppressed emotional wounds and deep-rooted emotionally charged unconscious beliefs that we carry, that we have learnt from hurtful life events. While these parts of us are unresolved they can become toxic and create unhealthy energy blockages that can also disrupt the vitality of the other energy bodies. Energy loss at this level can be due to toxic or unhealthy energy dynamics in relationships in which we become emotionally entangled, manipulated, or lost in another person or substance. We can also encounter energy loss at this level in shock or trauma, resulting in parts of our energy body being scattered out of our body, until signals are transmitted from our energy field that it is safe for those parts to return. This is a coping mechanism to numb ourselves while we are under harm, allowing us to have a disembodied response to cope with the traumatic event.

## THE VITALITY OF OUR MENTAL ENERGY BODY

The mental layer is the third layer of our energy field and pertains to our Fire element.

This layer of our energy body transmits the quality of our thoughts and feelings and the intensity of our will. Energy blockages of this energy body are often caused by our immediate train of thought, and any negative mental scripts that interfere with us actualising our power and potential. The integrity of this energy body can be compromised by low confidence and excess fear-based thinking and behaviour, that gets in the way of us manifesting our soul dream. The integrity of this energy body can also be lost in relationships where we give our power away, allowing our minds and paths to be programmed by the standards, needs and ideals of other people, groups or institutions.

---

## THE VITALITY OF OUR SPIRITUAL ENERGY BODY

The spiritual layer is the fourth layer of our energy field and corresponds to our Air element. The spiritual energy body is responsible for bringing the power of our awareness to our experience, so that we can bring more consciousness to the wholeness of our soul and the oneness of all there is. The spiritual energy body gives us conscious management and choice to evolve and expand. The more we bring our conscious awareness to our soul, the more we spiritually evolve towards our truth. Energy blockages of this energy body occur when we let our physical, emotional and mental blockages define our lives and who we are; resulting in an unlived soul life. Other blockages are unresolved wounds in our heart where a fundamental truth of who we are in our soul has been damaged or suppressed, leading to symptoms such as depression, addiction or feeling lost, disconnected and empty. Energy loss in this energy body occurs when we have a lack of faith in life and the universe, and contract into separation rather than expand into the whole. It often occurs when life events cause us to lose meaning and disrupt our spiritual connection to something greater than ourselves. Healing of the spiritual energy body involves shining the healing light of our awareness on to blockages and our lack of connection, to bring about resolution and spiritual evolution.

So, maintaining the vitality of all our energy bodies is tricky, huh? There are so many factors that can disrupt the vitality of our energy bodies and our connection to our soul in life. The important thing at this stage is to recognise if any of these energy imbalances or top-line symptoms resonate with your experiences, because then you can get a sense of what energy imbalances you would like to address in your crystal healing journey.

## THE CHAKRAS

Within our energy bodies there are energy channels through which life force is distributed around our bodies. Located along the central energy channel, we have seven primary energy centres, that are responsible for processing energy in different areas of our lives. These energy centres are called chakras. When we have an energy blockage or an energy loss, it is often reflected in the functioning of our chakras. As we address the root cause of an energy imbalance, crystals can be used to attune our chakras to restore a healthy distribution and flow of energy. Many crystals have an affinity with a particular chakra and energy body. Very generally speaking, we can choose a crystal for a chakra based on its colour, properties and our intuitive discernment of what might be right for us.

Descriptions of the chakras and a basic guide for selecting corresponding crystals are on the next page:

**The chakras**

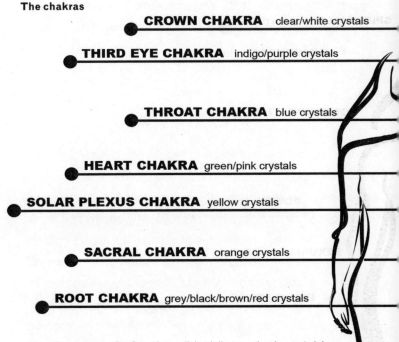

**CROWN CHAKRA** clear/white crystals

**THIRD EYE CHAKRA** indigo/purple crystals

**THROAT CHAKRA** blue crystals

**HEART CHAKRA** green/pink crystals

**SOLAR PLEXUS CHAKRA** yellow crystals

**SACRAL CHAKRA** orange crystals

**ROOT CHAKRA** grey/black/brown/red crystals

- Your **root chakra** (grey/black/brown/red crystals) grounds you physically and processes your survival and security. (Earth element)
- Your **sacral chakra** (orange crystals) processes your experiences of sensuality, sexuality, creativity and the emotions. (Water element)
- Your **solar plexus chakra** (yellow crystals) processes your sense of personal will, taking action and exerting your power in the world. (Fire element)
- Your **heart chakra** (green and pink crystals) processes your experience of compassion and love. It is also the gateway to the soul. (Air element)

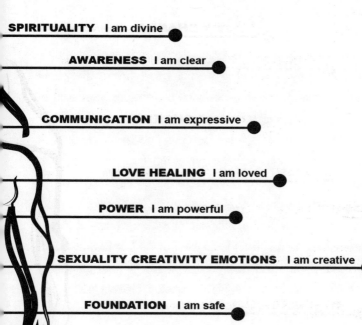

**SPIRITUALITY** I am divine

**AWARENESS** I am clear

**COMMUNICATION** I am expressive

**LOVE HEALING** I am loved

**POWER** I am powerful

**SEXUALITY CREATIVITY EMOTIONS** I am creative

**FOUNDATION** I am safe

- Your **throat chakra** (blue crystals) processes the dimensions of frequency, vibration, communication, and your ability to speak your truth. (Water element)
- Your **third eye chakra** (indigo/purple crystals) processes your ability to perceive and discern between possibilities in the quantum field, otherwise known as psychic seeing or divination. (Air element)
- Your **crown chakra** (clear/white crystals) connects you to the divine, and processes the power of your conscious awareness and your receptivity to transcendental experiences of awakening. (Air element)

## MAKING FRIENDS WITH TENSION

So now we know if we have an energy imbalance the intelligence of our being will always let us know through the subtle signs and symptoms we experience as tension; whether it be experienced physically, emotionally, mentally or spiritually.

Whether it be stress-related aches and pains, exhaustion, emotional overwhelm, anxiety, lack of meaning or low states of mind, most symptoms of tension are our energy body's way of communicating that there is an energy blockage or energy loss inside, and it is interfering with our connection to our soul and our flow of life force. It doesn't feel nice, but we just have to attend to the energy imbalance so that our soul can fluidly express itself in our life again and we can feel connected, present and whole.

However uncomfortable the top-line symptom of tension is, the tension is not the problem. Tension is the answer. It is the response of our being, nudging us to let us know it is time to reclaim lost parts of our self and give birth to the new. Tension is a sign that life is commanding a change and a new soul quality to come forth so that we can live our soul path. The quality and change exists in us; we just have to give birth to it. And giving birth is never easy. But it is all part of our journey for discovering our fullness.

We can either give in to the tension, fight it, dismiss it, or make friends with it and listen to the healing change it is seeking to bring forth in our consciousness.

Our soul has many parts, and many qualities. But energy imbalances may cause us to become too attached to the safety of one version of ourselves; we can become contracted in blockages and end up limiting the expression of our wholeness.

The self-correcting nature of life force will always give vitality to other parts of our soul that need to be expressed in our lives to counter-balance our one-sidedness. And as it pushes up against our blockages and our unconscious one-sided stance, the tension may feel really uncomfortable. But if we lean into our discomfort and give our tension room to reveal the underlying wisdom of the change that is seeking to be expressed in our lives, we can become something new. We can ask:

What is the tension trying to tell us about our lives?
What is the tension physically making us do? I.e. is it making you rest, stop what you're doing, stay awake, flee? Then find out why.
What lost or emergent part of our soul is trying to come through at this time?
What blockage or stagnant part of us is it time to release or integrate with the new?

There is wisdom in our tension. We just have to give ourselves the safe space to check in with how we are feeling, without fighting it or resisting it, but also without getting attached to or bogged down by it.

Sometimes we have to be lost to be found and tension acts just like a compass, providing us with direction, giving us an uncomfortable signal to tell us when we are going off track of our soul path. We have just forgotten how to read the compass and listen for the change our symptoms are asking of us.

This is where crystals come in. Crystals help us unlock the wisdom in our tension. When our tension gets overwhelming and we need a helping hand to understand what life is asking of us, crystals speak the language of energy, so that we don't have to. Sitting in meditation with crystals helps us to find a point of stillness to silence the clamour of the dissonance and channel the self-correcting nature of life force to restore harmony and the wisdom of the whole. By stilling our energy, meditation heightens the power of crystals to do their work of clearing our energy field of stagnant blockages that are incongruent to our soul dream; amplifying more soulful parts of ourselves so that we can meet life with more authenticity, strength and magic.

Across each element, crystals speak to qualities in our soul that need to come forth to fulfil that area of our lives. Crystals give our soul room to breathe, permission to express itself and a congruent frequency that will allow it to come through with grace and ease.

We experience the Earth element through the physical energy body, Water element through the emotional energy body, Fire through the mental energy body and Air through the spiritual energy body. When we are facing an energy imbalance in one of our energy bodies, we can refer to the Crystal Compass to help us restore harmony in that element.

Through relationships with crystals, you can deepen your intuitive relationship with yourself and with the rest of the universe. Everything in the universe is alive with spirit, including crystals, and the more you are in relationship with the spirit, the more you allow it into your life through the magical interconnectivity that is life.

Your journey with crystals invites in the rest of life to support you. As you align with your soul, you align with your soul's connection to the oneness with all that is. When you make a decision from your soul, the rest of the universe will hear you.

Working with crystals may spark synchronicities, happy meetings and transformative breakthroughs.

It may give you the courage you need to make the decisions that will best serve your wellbeing and soul path.

It may make you feel your truth, speak your truth and be your truth.

And it may free you to follow the intuitive way of life force to allow your soul's dreaming to come through.

## 2

# Identifying the Root of our Energy Imbalances

## TOXIC AND STAGNANT ENERGY

Toxic and stagnant energy is an energy frequency that is cut off from its soul, and therefore cut off from its source of life force energy. Once it is cut off from its source of vitality, it tends to become toxic and feed off other sources. When separated, toxic energy doesn't serve the whole, it only serves itself, polluting our spaces and adding a heaviness to the way we feel.

So, where does all this toxic and stagnant energy come from? Most of the time it comes from us.

Your soul is a dynamic composite of all your unique qualities, gifts and talents; it is your spiritual wholeness and highest service; it is the pure potentiality of who you are outside of time and space. There is no one quite like you. Your soul dreams of bringing forth and manifesting the totality of its potential qualities in this life or the next.

But when an expression of our soul enters the domain of our physical world, it enters the realm of duality; and it can be subject to life experiences that either thwart, distort or suppress its true nature. Did someone tell you not to be so loud? Or not to be so quiet? Or not to be so stupid? Whatever we have been told in our upbringing or adult life, there are so many ways in which we have had to edit the true nature of who we are. It is when our external environment interacts with our human management of our soul that our own expression of our soul qualities becomes inflicted with the inflation of our pride or the deflation of our pain, fears and self-doubt.

When the expression of our soul parts is distorted by an inflation or deflation, they can become separated from the intelligence of the whole, and start to work in manic isolation from each other, causing energetic dissonance and chaos in our energy field. We can experience this imbalance as confusion, inner conflict and other forms of tension, but we can often be totally unaware of it if it has become an unconscious way of being. As these parts of us become separated from the whole they tend to rob vitality from other parts of our being, causing an imbalance in our vitality distribution.

Other people's toxic energies are also flying around, draining or robbing vitality from other people. There can also be toxic energy in what we consume, whether that be food, drink or media. But before we address this we must take responsibility for our own toxic energies that are causing imbalances in ourselves. This will make us more impermeable to anyone else's toxic energy.

We can identify the main types of toxic energies through the narratives of the fear-based self.

## IDENTIFYING THE NARRATIVES OF THE FEAR-BASED SELF

The fear-based self is the fear-based part of us that is shaped by the world and our experiences. It is a very tender and vulnerable part of us, and what makes us human. It is also known as the ego but we can name it the fear-based self as it is a part of us that we have created from the protective mechanism of fear. It is the part of us that has become one-sided, conditioned by unresolved hurts that we have experienced from trauma, relationships, our upbringing or any life events that have knocked our spirit and caused pain in our heart.

Fear learns from life and while these wounds remain inside, unhealed and unintegrated with the soul, the fear-based self takes on beliefs from these experiences that affirm our separation rather than affirming our wholeness. The beliefs are based accordingly on a sense of lack or deficit, and commonly start with the wounded words: 'I'm not [insert quality here] enough.'

I'm not good enough, I'm not attractive enough, I'm not interesting enough, I'm not cool enough, I'm not enough. We all have one or two lurking.

From this deficit, we typically find the words 'should', 'must', 'need to', 'have to' ingrained into our psyche, driving behaviours that are constantly expending energy to compensate for our perceived inadequacies, to prove our worth, regain our self-esteem and win the approval of others:

'I should be more . . .'

'I shouldn't be . . .'

'I need to be more . . .'

'I have to be . . .'

'I must be . . .'

We can even start to take on roles or personas in our nego-tiation for love, acceptance or respect.

Other wounded deficit beliefs might involve a heightened sense of our separation, and sound like:

'I am alone.'

'I am rejected.'

'I am unlovable.'

'Nobody cares about me.'

'I have no one.'

'No one is there for me.'

Our wounded beliefs also make commentaries about the rest of the world. For example:

'All women/men are . . .'

'People are . . .'

'Everyone should . . .'

'If [something] . . . [something] this will happen.'

And sometimes a life experience could have been so trau-matic that we lose all faith and our baseline belief is that we just can't trust life. For example:

'The world is unsafe.'

'I am unsafe.'

'I don't trust anyone.'

The fear-based self, in its fear-based state, can also be a bit of a control freak too, trying to exert all the energy available to control, engineer and manage all aspects of life and all its outcomes, in fear of not being able to face the discomfort of uncertainty. The mind runs a million miles an hour and tension becomes rife in the body. It's exhausting. All are signs that the fear-based self is working overtime.

'I'll only be happy when . . .'

'Everything must work in this way for me to be OK . . .'

When the fear-based self is in overdrive with these constructs, and creating a one-sidedness in how we experience the world, it may be expending our energy in a stance that is contrary to our soul dream. The beliefs from unresolved wounds can cause a resistance to the soul's dreaming and create an imbalance in how we spend our energy. For example from a wounded space, we may easily give away our energy or pick up incongruent energies from others in unhealthy relationship dynamics that we have with people, things or the external environment.

The fear-based self isn't the enemy. It is a very tender and necessary part of who we are. We need it as our learning interface with the world. It is our vessel for energy, and its aim is to learn truths and come into wholeness so it can become a *true* mirror to the soul. The wounds of the fear-based self are not to be bypassed or dismissed, they are to be held and integrated, as a necessary part of discovering who we are.

But the fear-based self can be fierce and very savvy and, as a vehicle of separation, can sometimes think it knows best! How can we discern when we are operating from our fear-based self or true self? Remember, the fear-based self is the fear-based separated part of us that has not yet integrated with the soul. So, in its fear-based separation, its qualities are protective, defensive, competitive and needy as it tries to fill the void of the soul. It needs to be these things, because we genuinely need some of these qualities to survive. But until the wounds of the fear-based self have integrated with the soul, these competitive and defensive qualities will be operating in overdrive, with fear-based false beliefs causing elemental imbalance in our lives.

## BECOMING THE WHOLE SELF

The first thing in our crystal healing journey towards wholeness is to identify the fear-based narratives that are creating the energy blockages to your soul's dreaming. The following exercises help you to do that and identify what will be the best crystals in the compass to start with.

## EXERCISE 1: FEAR-BASED SELF WOUNDED BELIEFS

Use the table below to name some fear-based wounded beliefs that come to mind, that may be operating in you. Think of what you want to be and the voice that gets in the way of that – what does it say? Or name the narratives that parents, society or hurtful experiences have ingrained into you.

These are the energies that have become the background of your experience. They have become the energy from which you create your life and your relationships, the energy from which you live. They may be blocking the flow of your soul working in your life.

What is the energy you are living from? Creating from? Doing from? Relating from?

Is it from a space of fear or wholeness?

| WOUNDED BELIEFS | |
|---|---|
| Separation beliefs | Deficit beliefs and 'not enough' beliefs |
| Control freak beliefs | Beliefs about the world |

For separation beliefs, choose a crystal intuitively from the Air element that you feel would be most healing for this part of you.

For deficit beliefs and 'not enough' beliefs, use a Fire element crystal.

For control freak beliefs, use an Air element crystal such as aventurine, but again choose intuitively.

For beliefs about the world, choose a crystal from the Water element that would be most healing to that part of you.

Find a quiet space to begin a meditation holding the crystal you have chosen. Take a few deep breaths and centre yourself into a relaxed breathing rhythm, allowing your mind to quieten. Pay attention to your breathing and the way you feel until you notice the resonance of the crystal. Once you can sense a slight shift in your vibration and its effect in your energy field, ask:

1. What is the source of this wounded belief?
2. What soul part of me is this wounded belief suppressing?
3. What does the wounded part of me need to feel safe and healed?
4. What was my soul nature before this part of me was wounded?
5. How can I welcome these gifts back into my life and express them freely?
6. How are these gifts refined through this experience?
7. Are there any further crystals that will help this part of me?

We all have a bit of the 'control freak' and some uncon-scious wounded scripts inside, creating a space or an energy in us from which we perceive and live out our lives. Some of them we may be familiar with, like the ones we can name in the table, but more often than not we may be completely unconscious of them. They may be so automatic and so deeply ingrained in our psyche and behaviour that we have no conscious awareness that they are operating in our lives.

For those beliefs that are still unconscious, we can track them down by listening to other symptoms. Toxic energy will always give rise to symptoms of imbalance as it disrupts our energy distribution.

Check the Elemental Table (on the next page) to see if you can identify any common symptoms of imbalance that resonate with you. Then choose a crystal from that element to meditate with. In your meditation ask:

### What fear-based narrative is at the root of this imbalance?

Relax into the meditation. Do not force any answers, and just see what comes up. Even if nothing does come up, a process will have started for you.

Exercises in identifying the scripts of the fear-based self can be particularly powerful, as the simple act of naming them and bringing them into the light of your conscious awareness can withdraw power from them and start to deprogramme them from your energy field and unconscious mental patterns.

| ELEMENT | ENERGY BODY | AREAS OF OUR LIFE | RELATIONSHIP |
|---|---|---|---|
| **EARTH** | Body | Health<br>Stability<br>Home life<br>Career<br>Financial security | With our physical body, family and Mother Earth |
| **WATER** | Emotion | Emotional expression and wisdom<br>Intimacy<br>Intuition<br>Sensuality and sensory pleasure<br>Inspiration<br>Sexuality | With ourselves and others |
| **FIRE** | Mind | Power<br>Will<br>Confidence<br>Passion<br>Action<br>Fulfilling potential | With society and the world |
| **AIR** | Spirit | Faith<br>Love<br>Meaning<br>Purpose<br>Consciousness<br>Oneness<br>Spiritual life | With our soul and the divine |

| CHAKRA | IMBALANCES | |
| --- | --- | --- |
| | UNDERACTIVE | OVERACTIVE |
| Root (1st) | Exhaustion<br>Stress<br>Poor health<br>Adrenal fatigue<br>Financial or home issues | Overidentification with the body and material gain |
| Sacral (2nd)<br>Throat (5th) | Passive-aggression<br>Projection<br>Coldness<br>Depression<br>Numbness<br>Resentment<br>Stress<br>Anxiety | Overidentification with emotions<br>Addiction to sensory pleasures<br>Using emotions to manipulate others |
| Solar Plexus (3rd) | Powerlessness<br>Procrastination<br>Inaction<br>Indecision<br>Anxiety<br>Panic attacks<br>Low confidence and self-esteem<br>Mind easily controlled by others | Overidentification with power<br>Arrogance<br>Oppressive<br>Manipulation<br>Abusive<br>'Fiery'<br>Control freak<br>Racing or overactive mind |
| Heart (4th)<br>Third Eye (6th)<br>Crown (7th) | Lack of faith and meaning<br>Depression<br>Unlived soul life<br>Lost<br>Stuck in our head | Overidentification with spirituality<br>Spacey<br>Ungrounded<br>Delusional<br>Displaced<br>Rejection of the physical experience |

# 3

# Using Crystals

## GETTING STARTED

### WHERE TO SOURCE AND HOW TO CHOOSE CRYSTALS

Crystals are most widely available on the internet, and can also be purchased in specialist alternative healing shops. Make sure whoever you are purchasing your crystals from, you get a good vibe from them. If you are buying online be sure to see that the retailer has good reviews and that you get a good energy from their website or shop. I would avoid buying crystals that look synthetic or heat-treated. You can tell if crystals have been heat-treated if they look too deeply coloured.

All the crystals on the Compass are the most common and best-value stones, so they are readily available from most crystal retailers.

Crystals can be bought in their raw state or as tumbled stones. Use your intuition to decide and pick what form you'd prefer to work with. Both are equally effective. I personally prefer crystals in their raw state for my home, and tumbled stones for meditation and inner work.

Tumbled stones are great, because you can hold them in the palm of your hand comfortably during meditation, or keep them in your pocket or bag. They are also the most cost effective way of buying crystals.

The size of the stone does not matter; whether it be a very small tumbled stone or a large raw piece, the effects are the same. The most important thing is to follow your intuition to draw you to the right stone for you.

This book contains a selection of 40 crystals. There are many different stones in the world; I chose these 40 (41 if you include Clear Quartz) for their power, ability, strength, good value in terms of price, and availability.

These 40 stones are some of the most accessible and abundantly available stones, and they can change your world with their strengths and powers. I have all 41 in my primary toolkit, for myself and clients, like a first aid box. But just start with the ones you need. Don't go overboard! It's easy to do that with crystals! Just start with buying one or two or a few; make good use of the exercises to identify the stones you most need now and start there, and you will be well on your journey.

## CLEANSING YOUR CRYSTALS

Your crystals are energy conductors, and information keepers. They can become attuned with the energy that they have picked up from the environment or from a person. It is best to clean your crystals as often as you remember. I cleanse my crystals once a month. I recommend the following cleansing rituals.

- **Earth Crystals:** if you have a garden, bury your crystals in the earth, and ask Mother Earth to transmute their energy. Leave them overnight.
- **Water Crystals:** cleanse with water, preferably in a stream or natural body of water, and ask the body of water to neutralise the crystals of any energy they may have picked up. Water crystals can also become cleansed under the power of a full moon.
- **Fire Crystals:** leave them in the sun for up to half an hour and ask the sunrays to energise the crystal and transmute the energy they have picked up.
- **Air Crystals:** with the power of your conscious intention to cleanse the crystal, blow on the crystals stating your intention that with the power of the breath you neutralise the crystals of unwanted energy.

If you don't have a garden, don't fancy going to a stream, live somewhere where there's not much sun or just don't have time for this, you can use the cleansing breath method for all of them. But using crystals is all about relationship with the elements, so if you do have an opportunity to engage with nature in your cleansing rituals, I highly recommend it.

## CRYSTALS IN YOUR SPACE

Keep your crystals free of dust and somewhere you value as a sacred space. Or have them on proud display in your home, setting the intention for them to work their magic on bringing a quality of harmony or protection to the energy of your space.

# HOW TO USE CRYSTALS FOR HEALING

## MEDITATION

The best method of getting the most of crystals is to meditate with them. Meditation is the practice of bringing you conscious awareness to the present moment. Be in a comfortable sitting position. Sit so you are relaxed, yet upright. Take your crystal and place it in the centre of your hand placing your other hand on top of it. Breathe deeply, and settle your mind as you breathe in and out. Bring your conscious awareness to your breath, and then let your awareness spread to the signs and signals of your body. Just be the neutral awareness that notices what is arising, without judgement or attachment to an outcome. Be curious if you notice the resonance of your crystal. Notice what effect it is having on your body, emotions, mind and spirit. What energy are you feeling in your body? Allow yourself to continue to breathe deeply as you let the energy amplify in you.

When you are ready to end your meditation, ask yourself what quality the crystal has brought forth for you. Reflect on how you felt before and how you feel now, and notice if there is any difference. What insight i.e. what wisdom or gentle advice does the 'after meditation' you give to the 'before meditation' you? What would your life be like if you embodied this soul quality more?

## JEWELLERY

Wearing a crystal for long periods of time can be great to work on life patterns or themes that you want to consistently focus on. Crystal jewellery is also really pretty and will make you look and feel great! Bonus!

## CHAKRA MEDITATION

On pages 34-5 you'll see the chakra diagram, with their mantras. A crystal chakra meditation can be done by identifying a chakra you would like to work on. And intuitively choosing a crystal from its corresponding element.

Chakra meditations can be carried out like a normal meditation, but you can include the mantra that relates to that chakra as something to focus on or chant during your meditation. You can also choose to lie down in your meditation and place the crystal on your chakra.

If you'd like to work on all the chakras, I'd recommend a seven-day chakra meditation, where for each day of the week you do a meditation for each chakra, chanting each mantra, starting with the root chakra for day one and ending on the crown chakra for day seven.

Another means of chakra healing is by lying down in a quiet space and placing on each chakra a crystal of your choice that relates to that chakra. As you are lying down, make the intention that you are open to receiving universal life force energy and balancing of the chakras. This can be very restorative.

## EXERCISE 2: ENERGY AUDIT 1

On a scale of one to ten, for each quadrant choose a number, to score how fulfilled you feel you are in each element. This will give you an idea of what elements and crystals you need to work with the most. Do you feel any of your elements are overactive or underactive? There are questions included to help you reflect.

**Earth** – Body
How stable are your foundations? (Home/community/work/support network) How nourished is your physical body? How grounded do you feel?

**Fire** – Mind
Do you exert your power in the world towards your passion? Where do you give your power away? Who or what owns you? Where do you lose power? Who is winning, you or your fears? Do you feel empowered or powerless?

**Air** – Spirit
How connected do you feel to your soul? Do you wish for more meaning in your life? Are you being true to yourself?

**Water** – Emotion
How in touch are you with your emotions and intuition? Are you true to your emotions? Do you express them or let them go stagnant and toxic? Do you feel your emotions are balanced?

# USING CRYSTALS TO OVERCOME TENSION OR LIFE PATTERNS

Energy imbalances or blockages can manifest in feelings of tension or life patterns. We can choose a crystal from the Compass, based on the area of our life and the energy body the tension or life pattern relates to. Here are two quick-fix guides to using the Compass for overcoming energy imbalances and life patterns.

## EXERCISE 3: CHOOSING A CRYSTAL FOR AN ENERGY IMBALANCE

- Follow the signals of the soul dream, by honouring and listening to all parts of your being. Check in with the way you feel in each energy body.
- Name the issue or tension you are experiencing; bring your conscious awareness to the sensation, without resistance, and identify what quality needs to come through to ease this tension.
- Choose a crystal from the Compass that will bring through this quality and choose an exercise or a way of working with the crystal that will help.
- Be conscious of what change this quality is asking of you in your life.

## EXERCISE 4: MEDITATION FOR LIFE PATTERNS

Find a quiet space within choosing a crystal relating to a life pattern you would like to address.

Bring your conscious awareness to the pattern that is no longer serving you and that you wish to evolve from.

- What is the nature of the life pattern?
- When and with whom does it occur in your life?
- What element does this life pattern relate to?
- Close your eyes and check in with the energy body that is related to this element.
- Bring your conscious awareness to the signs and signals being communicated through this energy body when you think about this life pattern. What do you feel? How do you feel? Where do you feel it? What are the thoughts, emotions, or sensations?
- What energy are you operating from when you engage in this life pattern? Is it one of wholeness or deficit? What are you seeking when you are engaged in their life pattern? Describe the role you are playing and how you use your energy. How do you lose energy?
- What wounded belief does this life pattern come from?
- Ask the crystal to amplify your soul dream that is emerging that seeks to heal this wounded belief and overcome this life pattern. Ask what strengths and

qualities are trying to come through in your life to overcome this life pattern. What advice is trying to come through to counter-balance this pattern? What healing quality does this original wound or unconscious belief need?

• Are there other crystals from the Compass that will help you bring forth this quality in your life?

Be conscious of what change this quality is asking of you in your life and what change the quality will bring into your life.

## EXERCISE 5: HOW TO FIND SOUL DREAM WISDOM IN TENSION

Let us take as a premise that the purpose of energy healing is to transmute tension and unlock the soul wisdom behind it that will enable you to reclaim power and walk your soul path. To help us discern between the emergent soul wisdom and the old narratives of the fear-based self within the tension, a quartz crystal can be used. Energy that has gone toxic or stagnant in the fear-based self will feel heavy and difficult. In contrast, the soul's wisdom will feel light, connected and effortless and we will feel a sense of relief when we embody it in our lives. To help us discern between the two, we can programme a quartz crystal to help us.

# PROGRAMMING YOUR DIAGNOSTIC QUARTZ CRYSTAL

## CHOOSING A CRYSTAL

You can use any quartz crystal for this exercise. It could be a small tumbled stone, or a medium or large raw piece. The important thing is to let your intuition decide. To choose your quartz crystal intuitively, surrender the dominance of the mind and let your body guide you towards choosing one. Let your fingers intuitively lead you to the one that will work for you.

## CLEANSING THE CRYSTAL

Cleanse the crystal with water, preferably in a natural body of water such as a river or a stream, but under a tap will also do. While you are washing the crystal, make your intention either in your mind, or out loud: 'I am washing this crystal with the intention of cleansing it.'

Once you intuitively know it is cleansed, trust your knowing, and dry the crystal.

Then blow on it with your breath, with the intention of cleansing it of any energies that are not aligned to you.

## PROGRAMMING THE CRYSTAL

Close your eyes and take a few deep breaths to still the mind and slow the body down. Then become very clear in your intention, with full power, stating: 'I programme this crystal to act as my soul dream diagnostic tool.'

Say this in your inner mind as many times as feels right for you. Say it with full power until you feel it is done. Trust your knowing. And then give thanks to the crystal, stating: 'It is done.'

## MAINTAINING YOUR CRYSTAL

I recommend cleansing and programming your crystal every month. It can be very helpful to coordinate your cleansing of the crystal with the moon cycle. A full moon is a potent day for clearing your crystal of any energies that you are not aware of. A new moon can be a potent day for programming your crystal with new intentions or repeat intentions to strengthen its power.

## FINDING SOUL DREAM WISDOM EXERCISE

Choose a physical, emotional, mental or spiritual tension that you are experiencing right now or that you often experience. The art of knowing how your intuition talks to you through tension, requires you to get really descriptive with what is going on in the body. While doing the exercise, really tune in to what is going on so you can attain the full intelligence of what is being communicated. More than anything, the important thing is to describe the energy. That means describing the quality of what is going on.

### STEPS

If you are using a diagnostic quartz, have it ready by your side, as you will be using it in step 3.

First, take a few moments and really connect with how you are feeling and tap into the tension head on, with bravery, without resistance, knowing in your heart that the tension is a guide to your true self. Then deepen into the intelligence of the tension. Find your resistance to the tension. We always have a resistance – a little bit of aversion to our tension – because it doesn't feel nice, so we may have aversion tactics. What are yours? Ignoring the tension? Denying it? Distracting yourself from it? Trying to'fix it with something else? Or tensing up even more in an attempt to protect yourself from it? Once you have found your resistance, take a deep breath, release your resistance and dive into it and begin.

1. **Name the tension:** How does the tension manifest? What effect is it having on you? Describe what it feels like. How does your tension communicate with you emotionally, physically and mentally? Close your eyes to really describe your energy and how everything feels.

2. **Identify the opposing energy:** Name what you are thinking, feeling, doing at the point you are feeling this tension.

   a. Thinking: What is the narrative of your train of thought, what is the energy of the thoughts? Notice any thoughts that are emotionally loaded, have a sense of pressure, pain, insecurity or entitlement e.g. 'I need to…', 'I should be…', 'He should be…' Are the thoughts controlling, judgemental, needy, angry? Really get a sense of the energy of the thoughts.

   b. Feeling: Describe the mood of what you are feeling – are you feeling low, tired? Are you frustrated? How are you feeling emotionally? How are you feeling energetically? Do you feel present? Or away with the fairies?

   c. Doing: What is your behaviour in this moment? What

are you actually doing? What is the energy of what you
are doing? Is it rushed, is it manic? Is it slow and forced?

3. **Tap into your soul dream:** Pick up your diagnostic
   quartz and ask that it amplify your soul wisdom. Start
   breathing into your heart chakra. Let go of your attachment
   to anything identified in step 2. Make the intention to lean
   into what makes the tension uncomfortable. What is my
   discomfort trying to tell me? What about those feelings is
   not true to me or not serving my heart? What does the pull
   of my soul dream want instead?

4. **Resolution:** What actions can I take to come into
   resolution and follow the soul dream guidance? What
   healing needs to happen in me to transmute the energy in
   step 2 so I can reclaim myself and honour my heart's call
   for resolution? Identify the elements that need to be worked
   on and use the Crystal Compass to identify the crystals
   that can help you with that.

| OPPOSING ENERGY | TENSION | SOUL DREAM |
|---|---|---|

**Thinking:** Dominant
train of thought or belief.

**Feeling:** What is the
underlying feeling or
emotion?

**Doing:** What is your
predominant behaviour?
What is the energy of
your behaviour?

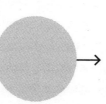 ← →

# CASE STUDY

Client A was up one night with insomnia. She was desperate to get to sleep, as she had an early start and a lot of work to do the next day. Her desperation to get to sleep was her resistance to the tension. She said, 'Okay, this isn't working. Rather than forcing the intelligence of my body to do something else, I'm going to go with my body wanting to be awake for a moment.' She switched the light on, grabbed her diagnostic crystal that it was by her side and took a few deep breaths, releasing her resistance to the tension.

1.  She began by naming the tension – how was it manifesting? Well, the first one was insomnia, and she generally felt the tension manifesting as a feeling of being on edge. There was an energy of uncertainty and a feeling of being unclear, and her mind was racing.

2.  She identified the opposing forces.

## Thinking:

*Friend issues:* She had had an ongoing disagreement with a friend: she felt annoyed at her friend at something she had said to her at dinner the other night. She felt her friend was judging her and was condescending about the way she had handled a situation at work, but she didn't say anything at the time, because she didn't want the confrontation. But the comments had been quite energetically loaded and had stayed with her. The client's thoughts were repetitively playing out scenarios where she could redeem herself and look great, so she could prove the friend wrong and let the friend know subliminally that she was being judgemental.

*Work issues:* The client was also feeling overwhelmed at work, and noticed that there were a lot of thoughts that said, 'I'm not doing a good job, I'm not good enough at my job, everyone is going to think the project I'm working on is awful.' There were also a few emails that she hadn't replied to for over a week, that she kept putting off, because she was so overwhelmed – that was also playing on her mind. She didn't realise that all of this was going on in her head until she wrote down: 'What are the thoughts keeping me up?'

## Feeling:

She felt agitated by the friend issue, tight and pressured in her chest by the expectations she had placed on herself at work, and guilty about the emails.

## Doing:

Apart from trying to sleep, she was also trying to work out situations through which she could redeem herself, through imaginary scenarios where she could 'prove' herself, but the energy of this 'doing' was from a space of insecurity and lack of self-belief.

3. Tapping into the soul dream: She picked up her crystal, breathed into her heart and leant into her tension more, asking, 'What does the intelligence of this tension want? What does the soul dream want?'

She found: 'I am being kept awake to resolve all this activity, because it needs to get resolved, and put to bed, so I can go to bed! I don't really want to prove to my friend that I'm doing great and she is too judgemental, I just want to tell her how I feel. And in the long run, I don't want to let her judgemental nature affect me so much. Why do I care so much about what she thinks of me? I care because I am insecure about myself and the choices I make. I want to have more integrity and trust the work that I do, and the choices that I make. Integrity and being true to my word is important to me – not just for others, but for me and trusting myself. I want to manifest this more in my life.'

4.  Resolution: 'The first thing I'm going to do as soon as I wake up, before I do anything else, is email those people I have been avoiding. I am not going to put so much pressure on trying to be perfect in my response to emails to the point where I blow the work of them out of proportion and end up avoiding them. I am going to be brave and mention to my friend about how I felt after her comment. I am going to work on reclaiming my power from all the people I have given my power away to, whose approval my insecurities need. I am going to work on healing my neediness for approval and build my confidence and self-belief. I am going to manifest more integrity and trust in my life.'

After the client had reached this clarity, her tension eased and she fell asleep. This client fulfilled all the tasks she received in her soul dream guidance, and chose to work with crystals of golden apatite to improve her confidence and trust in her decisions and blue lace agate to speak her truth.

In order to reclaim her power and to feel confident, she used a golden heliodor crystal; to speak her truth, she used a turquoise crystal.

## OPPOSING ENERGY

**Thinking:**
Running through scenarios to prove friend wrong. Worried about not doing a good job at work, worried about not having integrity and about being unreliable.

**Feeling:**
Agitated, anxious, guilty, low in confidence, overwhelmed.

**Doing:** Trying to sleep! But also trying to prove herself through imaginary scenarios.

**TENSION**

INSOMNIA
FEELING ON EDGE
MIND RACING
UNCERTAINTY
FEELING UNCLEAR

**SOUL DREAM**

Honour my integrity.
Reclaim power from neediness for approval of others.
Trust my decisions.
Build confidence.
Speak my truth.

# 4

# Earth

*I nourish the gift of my body and establish firm foundations
in this world to survive and thrive in harmony with Mother Earth.*

Earth, our home; the beautiful planet that hosts our experience. Earth element is our primary element and our foundation in life. It gives us the physical body and physical life itself, and its vitality rewards us with the strength, health and security to survive and thrive.

## AREA OF LIFE

Earth element is the essence of matter and signifies establishing a strong foundation in our home life, career and in the immediate network we call our family and community. It is also our primary relationship to Mother Earth herself; how we relate to her, how we cope with life on her terrain, how we give thanks for her gifts.

Earth element is not so much about mastery of our environment, but more about becoming one with our environment and taking our place in the great ecosystem of the planet.

## NOURISHING THE VITALITY OF THE PHYSICAL ENERGY BODY

Earth element represents our physical body; the beautiful, intelligent vessel that houses our spirit. The body is amazing. It is an ecosystem in itself; a complex, self-regulating symphony of cosmic intelligence and a perfect miracle of many parts operating as a whole.

Our physical energy bodies are perhaps the most precious, complex and fundamental parts of all the energy bodies, because they are the foundation from which we can evolve to our truth.

The body needs love, shelter, nutrition, clean water, sleep and rest, movement, sunlight, nature, the elements and the sacred act of breathing. The breath is our beginning, and is how life force enters our body to be circulated to every cell in our being. Sometimes we can forget just to breathe and fill ourselves with the most abundant and on-tap source of life force. To breathe consciously and deeply is to reset and refuel with the self-correcting intelligence of life force, and to centre ourselves in its wisdom. To stop and consciously breathe in any situation can make the difference between an out-of-control reaction and a conscious response on our soul path.

Working with crystals gives us some respite and clarity to breathe. Crystals can elevate us out of daily survival mode and refresh our perspective with the eyes of the soul, to give us a deep knowing of what we need to do to transform our world. They can help us address deep-rooted limitations in our energy body, such as ancestral patterns and limiting beliefs, that may be compounded by the challenges of our surroundings.

How do we make room in our lives to listen to the intelligent symphony of our physical energy body? Is it in harmony or is there a dissonance? And how can we respond to the dissonance to elicit the change that our body may be asking of us? How can we listen more to our body's needs?

## SYMPTOMS OF EARTH ELEMENT IMBALANCES

There are many signs, symptoms and life patterns that can indicate Earth element imbalances. Weak Earth element can manifest as low energy, exhaustion, poor health, feeling frazzled, not feeling safe in the world or having to live in a constant state of fight or flight, due to financial insecurity or instability in our career or home life. Excess Earth element occurs when we become overly identified with material things. We become dependent on material gain to reward us with happiness. Or we become greedy or vain, as we overidentify with our physical form and the acquiring of more stuff. It can lead us to neglect our spiritual inner life and lead to a disconnect between our body and soul. If you have strong Earth or identify with excess Earth symptoms, you may benefit more from crystals in the other elements to restore a more balanced distribution of vitality across the neglected energy bodies.

# EARTH ELEMENT IN OUR LIVES

**Energy body:** Physical energy body.

**Element qualities:** Physical health and vitality, stability, security, safety, survival, firm foundations.

**Areas of our life:** Home life, career, financial security.

**Relationships:** Family, community, Mother Earth.

**Chakras:** Root (1st).

**Physical body areas:** Blood, bones, base of spine, legs, feet.

**Energy body vitality needs:** Breath, shelter, safety and warmth, nutrition, clean water and hydration, rest and sleep, movement, sunlight, access to nature.

**Energy body vitality loss causes:** Self-neglect, stressful, unstable or unsafe environments, rejection of the body and the physical experience, ancestral patterns around money, abuse and ill health, suppressed issues in the emotional, mental or spiritual energy body that drain energy distribution from physical energy body.

**Energy imbalance symptoms:**

*Underactive Earth*: Low energy and physical exhaustion, low immune system, stress and stress-related illnesses, poor circulation, poor health, disconnected from body (especially lower back, legs and feet), ungrounded or spacey, fight or flight anxiety (chronic fear and worry about survival, e.g. money, safety etc), life patterns of financial insecurity, housing issues or career issues.

*Overactive Earth*: Vanity and overidentification with the body, greed and overly driven by material gain.

## EXERCISE 6: CHECKING IN

Having read about Earth element, check in with yourself and see what resonated for you. On a scale of one to ten, rate how fulfilled and balanced you feel in your Earth element. Reflect on questions such as:

How stable are your foundations? (Home/community/
work/support network)

How nourished is your physical body?

How grounded do you feel?

Where are you losing vitality?

Where can you reclaim vitality?

Note down your reflections here:

## EXERCISE 7: RECLAIMING VITALITY OF OUR PHYSICAL ENERGY BODY

Energy loss leads to imbalance. Where are we losing vitality and connection to our soul? These exercises allow us to identify relationships, environments, conditioning or life events that are at the root of an energy blockage or energy loss; so we can then choose a crystal to help us reclaim that part of our self.

| ELEMENT | Energy imbalance symptoms and life patterns<br><br>E.g. poor health, stress-related illness | Causes<br><br>E.g. stressful environments |
|---|---|---|
| **EARTH**<br>Physical energy body | | |

## EXERCISE 7A: VITALITY LOSS AND HEALING ORIGINAL WOUND

Did you recognise any physical energy vitality loss symptoms in your life? What might be the root causes of these symptoms? Use the descriptions in the 'energy body vitality loss causes' section of the box on page 74 to help you. Note down what resonates in the grid below, write freely. Holistic healing seeks to address the root cause of the symptom, rather than the symptom itself, allowing for a true healing and transformation. Once you have identified causes in your life, choose a crystal from the Compass in the Earth element that will support you to overcome these issues.

| What action can I take to support this part of me? What changes can I make in my environment to support me? | Which crystals from the Compass will help me reclaim my physical vitality? Which crystals from the Compass will help me to overcome life patterns related to Earth element imbalances? |
|---|---|
|  |  |

## EXERCISE 7B: RELATIONSHIP AUDIT

Reflect on the quality of your relationships with key aspects of your Earth element. Assess if your current relationship with these aspects in your life is nourishing or depleting your physical vitality. Assess if your current relationship serves your soul dream and whether it is a fear-based relationship or a wholeness-based relationship. Answer intuitively and freely.

| Relationship | Nourishes energy? | Depletes energy? | Serves soul dream? | Fear-based se relationship or wholeness relationship? |
|---|---|---|---|---|
| Home life | | | | |
| Career/ current job | | | | |
| Your community | | | | |
| Physical body | | | | |

| Crystal insight meditation resolution: How can this relationship become more balanced? How might I reclaim myself both internally and externally? What actions do I need to take? | Which other crystals from the Compass might support you on your healing journey? |
| --- | --- |
| | |
| | |
| | |
| | |

# EXERCISE 7C: EARTH SELF-CARE NOURISHMENT OF VITALITY

|  | **AUDIT** |
| --- | --- |
| Self-nurturing and self-care | How much do you nurture your body? (1–10) |
| Presence | How present are you in your body? (1–10) |
| Groundedness | How embodied do you feel?<br>How connected to all parts of your body do you feel?<br>How connected to Mother Earth do you feel?<br>Is your vitality being evenly distributed throughout the body? |
| Stability and security | How stable is your financial and home life? |

## CRYSTAL RESOLUTION

Reflect on the sources of vitality nourishment such as food, water, exercise, rest, access to nature etc. What can you do more of to nurture the vitality of your physical energy body? Which crystals can support you on that journey?

Use an Earth crystal of your choice to call back all your attention and awareness to the present moment.

Spend some time in meditation to call to any parts of your vitality that are lost in another time or place, in the past, future or other spiritual planes of existence.

Ask the crystal for help to find insight into what needs to be resolved in your timeline to keep you present and at your most vital.

Choose a grounding crystal from the Earth element to ground your energy, and ask your soul dream to guide you on being more grounded in your life.

What are your desires for your financial and home life? What crystals can help you amplify soul qualities to manifest that?

# Energising

## PYRITE

Get up and go!!! Yeaaaaaah!!

Pyrite works on enlivening the body, preparing it for action; it gets the blood flowing and corrects your energy field so that your vitality is evenly distributed around the body. Pyrite reclaims any energy that is being wasted in tense muscles or fear-based thoughts, and makes that energy available for getting on with more useful things that are aligned to your soul dream. It is very efficient like that, and so will you be after a few moments of meditation with a piece.

Are you feeling sluggish? Lazy? Hungover? Or are you just really putting off something like going to the gym, studying, or any activity you just can't quite conjure up the energy to face, siding with the thought, 'I can't be bothered', when really in your heart, you know you should. There are often conflicting parts in us; one that wants to do something good, and one that would rather stay in bed. If you have made a commitment in your heart to doing something that is going to serve your well-being, but there is a part of you in the way of that, pyrite is your man for the job. And I say man, because pyrite has a divine masculine energy of order and action.

Pyrite makes you look alive and engages your total body and vitality in the commitment you've made. Pyrite will give you the upright 'can do' attitude you need to do the things that might be a little hard physically or mentally, but ultimately accomplishing these things will nourish you and make you feel good. Pyrite cuts through the fears of getting started on something, helping you realise the thing you were worried about starting was really not that hard to get into after all.

Ultimately pyrite raises your vitality. It conducts a very orderly type of energy. It will activate your energy in a grounded, systematic and embodied way. Rather than a crazy high, it offers a balanced and sustained lift that will last the duration of the task at hand.

Try a meditation with pyrite instead of coffee in the morning. Whereas coffee quickens up the mental faculties where you need a lift, pyrite is a total-body experience and enlivens the whole body in a more evenly distributed way; without the coffee crashes, or the manic-brain-working-overtime caffeine side effects.

Pyrite has a refreshing effect, and can make you feel like a load has been lifted; literally this is often the case, as pyrite is very efficient at releasing heavy energy blocks that have been draining your vitality. Often energy blockages disrupt our electromagnetic field, causing disharmony in the flow of energy around our body and the way we feel. These disruptions can lead to more chronic symptoms that indicate that the energy blockages have taken over to the degree that they are affecting our physical health and wellbeing. Regular use of pyrite may be of help in speeding up the body's natural healing process by getting rid of the contributing factors.

Balancing our electromagnetic field has the effect of connecting us to the spiritual essence above, yet grounding us in the magnetic field of Mother Earth below. This allows life force energy to flow through us freely, giving us an additional vitality boost, and aligning our physical bodies to take action in manifesting our soul dream.

Pyrite is the ultimate vitality stone. It is a great stone for good health and giving you that extra kick when you need it.

**Qualities:** Energising, efficiency, refreshing, grounding, willpower, taking action, mental and physical strength, balancing energy field, divine masculine principle.

**Good for:** Studying, working on a big project, exercising, manifesting soul dream, getting on with it, early mornings, releasing tense muscles that are contracting in fear of doing work, giving up coffee.

**Issues:** Procrastination, sluggishness, laziness, hangovers, bad habits, having too many ideas and not putting them into action, early morning haziness.

**Mantra:** I love life, let's do this!

# Grounding

## HEMATITE

Away with the fairies? Or feeling energetically scattered across the universe? Hematite pulls you back into the roots of your being at the base of your spine, grounding your energy back in your body. Hematite is very strong and has an almost gravitational effect of pulling you back to terra firma.

If you are feeling spacey or out of sorts, hematite is the crystal for you. It is particularly useful if you have experienced an out-of-body experience or a shock or a trauma, which has knocked your spirit out of you. If you have never felt the same since that shock or trauma, in that you feel like you are still not all here, hematite used with opal will help you to call that part of you, to gently return back into your body.

Hematite is even effective to use after high states of panic. Often in panic attacks, it can feel like we lose ourselves, and become dispersed into the ether. Hematite centres us and brings us back to earth.

Being grounded is about being rooted in the earth and in your earthly experience, but it is also about being present. If you are finding it difficult to stay present and keep your attention on the now, hematite can get your head out of the clouds, and restore parts of your attention that may be lost in the memories of the past, or fantasies or anxieties of the future. Hematite calls you back to the present and grounds you in the tasks at hand.

—

Hematite works on the central energy channel of your body or the sushumna, as it is known in Sanskrit. The sushumna acts as a pathway for energy to travel, and runs up the length of your spinal cord, progressing through the chakras. Hematite strengthens the functioning of the sushumna, making hematite a great crystal for general spinal health. Hematite supports healthy flow of vitality through the central energy channel, which is not only great for our health and all-round functioning of the chakras, it also primes us for having natural kundalini experiences depending on our needs and path of development.

Kundalini is a dormant energy at the base of our spine. It is an intelligent source of primal vitality. Kundalini is said to bring about our formation in the womb and connects us to life force. In our daily lives kundalini remains latent, coiled up like a snake in the base of our spine to hold our energy field in stasis; but it can rise up the central energy channel during different experiences of spiritual or energetic awakenings, giving us a sensory experience of the joy of life force rising through our energy bodies.

On a physical level, hematite is known as a detoxifier. It is also a tonic for the blood flow, so is energetically beneficial for illnesses or conditions concerning the blood.

**Qualities:** Grounding, presence, practicality.
**Good for:** Detoxing, embodying soul qualities and gifts, manifesting soul dream, calling back lost parts of the energy body.

**Issues:** Spaced out, panic attacks, trauma, out-of-body experiences, not being present, blood-related health issues, poor circulation, back/spinal issues, bad posture.

**Mantra:** I am here, I am safe and I am loved on terra firma.

# Rejuvenation

## MOOKAITE (MOOK JASPER)

You are as young as you feel; mookaite restores a carefree youth at heart, helping you to look and feel young again.

Mookaite has the power to rejuvenate our vitality both spiritually and physically. It is a stone of cosmic rebirth and can make you feel like a fresh new spirit. This makes it a great stone for releasing the weight of your past, and fearlessly leaping into new beginnings.

Energetically, mookaite has a tonifying effect on your energy field in that it boosts your available energy with life force in the areas that need it most. It is a particularly good stone to use for rest and renewal, after a period of hard work or exhaustion, to help you feel refreshed and like yourself again.

Mookaite revitalises the body to boost your physical and mental performance, so it can make you very sharp and vibrant. This makes it great for things like quick thinking, decision-making, as well as boosting your memory and alleviating forgetfulness. If you've forgotten something, such as a PIN number, something you were supposed to do that you can't quite remember, or where you put your keys, get quiet, hold some mookaite and see what comes up.

Mookaite restores youthful vigour and can counter-balance the effects of premature ageing caused by energy imbalances derived from stress, emotional blockages, interferences or chronic anxieties.

If you have become quite serious in life and 'old before your time', mookaite can assist you to liven up your world with more spontaneity and adventure.

Mookaite is a good stone for connecting to your soul, in a very grounded and embodied way. It helps you remember the immortal vibrancy of the soul, which is outside of time and space and removed from the earthly experience of ageing.

As a stone associated with birth and rebirth, and the moment of incarnation, mookaite can support with healing any traumas around birth or past lives. It can also be used for boosting memories of past lives.

Mookaite is from the Jasper family of crystals. Most Jaspers are great at reviving the physical energy body. Try Red Jasper to get the blood moving when you need to feel refreshed and ready for action.

**Qualities:** Rejuvenation, revitalising, renewal, invigorating, spontaneity, youthfulness, free-spirited, carefree, trusting the knowing of your soul, birth, rebirth.

**Good for:** Jumping into new adventures/new beginnings, connecting with soul, strengthening the memory, remembering past lives, healing birthing traumas or past lives, reversing premature ageing, brightening skin tone, brightening complexion and eyes, risk-taking, carefree decision-making, pregnancy.

**Issues:** Forgetfulness, premature ageing, exhaustion, depletion, being too serious, stress, fears around ageing.

**Mantra:** Life is for living!

---

# Health

## JADE

Health is wealth, and jade is *the* stone for good health and vitality.

Jade is one of the most revered and cross-culturally valued stones in history. Uses of jade stretch back to prehistoric China, India, South East Asia, the Pacific Islands and Meso-America.

Holding jade may give you an immediate sense of why it has been so widely valued. Jade strengthens your physical vitality by increasing life force throughout the body. The more you are connected to life force energy, the more you become a channel for its self-correcting intelligence. Life force energy can work through you at the level that is needed for you, helping to correct the energy distribution in the physical body, to restore a healthy vibration and flow. Jade maximises this effect.

Jade holds the frequency of Mother Earth and nature, which is innately governed and connected to life force in its connection to the whole.

It is why nature is so healing for us when life gets crazy. Have you ever spent time in nature and felt refreshed? Rejuvenated? Or revived? Nature reconnects us to the original wisdom of life force, and lets its balancing force back into our lives.

This is why ancient people have so deeply revered and respected nature and its divine connection to the whole, and have always sought to work in alliance with the delicate balance of the natural world, rather than against it.

Jade carries the energy signature of the natural world, and keeping a piece with you connects you to that natural power; it invites the harmony and vitality of the natural world into your life, to help you find inner and outer balance, and to nourish your overall health, wealth and wellbeing. Jade is a stone of wealth because it is in alignment with the abundance of nature.

When life brings you chaos, jade brings you balance; if work life is excessively stressful, keeping jade with you may help you find the work–life balance you are looking for.

Jade reminds you to take care of yourself and your heavenly body, but also to take care of the natural environment that hosts your existence. Jade allows life force to amplify your soul dream, so that whatever it is you do in this life, you are living out your unique service to the whole.

Jade brings the vibration of Mother Earth into your energy field; a natural and loving energy that is holistically healing and strengthening to your overall health and happiness. If you are somebody who lives in the city, with limited access to nature, having jade can be highly beneficial, to help nourish the vitality of your physical energy body. Along with food, water, movement, love and shelter, connection to nature and the elements is one of our basic needs for health.

Jade helps you deepen your relationship with the natural world, so that it can become your teacher, healer, ally and friend, and you can call on nature to cooperate in your united efforts to manifest what is true for you and true for the whole.

This can reward you with deep meaning, connection and

happiness on your earth journey and awaken you to earth's magic.

**Qualities:** Health, wealth, balance, harmony, earth's love
and magic.

**Good for:** Reconnecting with nature, attracting abundance,
finding work–life balance.

**Issues:** Busy, crazy city life, poor health and vitality.

**Mantra:** Earth is magic, and so am I. I feel nature's health,
harmony and abundance in my being.

# Protection

## OBSIDIAN

You know what, it is not all love and light. This is a universe of polarities, and sometimes people want to do you wrong. They want to throw bad mind vibes your way to harm or upset you.

Obsidian is like a wicked witch who has your back. She protects the most vulnerable spots of your energy field, namely the back of your neck and your heart. When people throw daggers your way, those are the most usual points of entry to influence your energy field. Obsidian gives you an iron-like protective cloak on your back, so that the energy of other people's stuff will not be able to penetrate.

Obsidian gives you an upright strength in your body that will deflect even the toughest of interferences seeking to harm you. Interferences are any type of vitality-draining energies that steer you away from the light of your soul dream. They can come from environments, people, entities that carry heavy attachments or social pressures from media that embed moods or unconscious thought patterns in you that get in the way of your highest path.

Take obsidian with you if you feel you may be entering a toxic environment or are having to spend time with somebody you find has a toxic impact on you.

Having a piece of obsidian on a pendant that you wear to hang down your back under a top can by a great ally for protecting you in difficult interactions.

—
93

We can be more vulnerable to picking up negative energy when we have had a high intake of alcohol or other stimulants. Stimulants can disrupt the energy distribution in the body, and on occasion can displace our own energy from out of our body, making us vulnerable to other energy. Using obsidian after a heavy night can help to ground us back in our body, to reclaim our space and draw out anything heavy or unsavoury that may have stayed with us.

If your home life has been threatened, obsidian is a great stone to keep at your front door as a means of protecting your home's energy field.

Obsidian is good to use if there is someone in particular that you feel brings negative energy into your life. It is good to contemplate with obsidian to understand the nature of the relationship, and if this person is nourishing your soul dream. If they are not, then what action or shift is this relationship requiring? Obsidian screens out their influence over you so that you can reclaim your body and think clearly about how to change the relationship.

Is there someone who has a hold over you, someone you can't appear to shake off or get out of your head, even though you know they are not good for you? Perhaps an ex-lover or someone you have had a close relationship with. Working with obsidian over a long period of time in meditation and visualisation can help you cut the energy cords that allow this person still to have influence over your life. If you can't seem to clear this person from your being, and you feel part of them is still with you and part of you is still with them, meditating with obsidian can help you communicate with the spiritual nature of your relationship with this person, giving you the insight to reclaim yourself and clear your energy field of that person's energy. This may take some time, but obsidian will help you to get to the bottom of the issue, so that you can clean it out of your life and grow from it.

Obsidian works on cleaning up the remnants of toxic energies from the physical body that come from frequencies such as spite, resentment, passive-aggression or shaming. Whether they are your own or someone else's, obsidian has a strong ability to pull old remnants of them out of your field of influence.

As long as people have negative thoughts, whether about themselves or others, there will always be negative thought forms emanated into the atmosphere wherever we go. The more in our power we are and the more we occupy our bodies, the less likely it is that energy in the environment is going to affect us. Either way, if you are feeling vulnerable, obsidian is your guy.

There is always a spiritual lesson to negative encounters, so while we can protect ourselves from them, it is useful to find out what the root causes may be for us or understand what the spiritual lessons are. Obsidian won't just help protect you, but will also help you rebuild your vitality and spiritual insight to grow and evolve from these threats.

**Qualities:** Protection, grounding, cleansing.
**Good for:** Difficult conversations, detoxing after a night out,

cutting energy cords from past relationships that are still in your energy field.

**Issues:** Toxic environments, toxic relationships.

**Mantra:** By the protective power of my wicked witch, no negative energy can enter my energy field.

# Strength

## ONYX

Onyx releases vitality into our muscles, helping us to feel at our most powerful and strong. When something requires us to use the strength of our physical body, onyx is a good stone to meditate with beforehand to channel the vitality of our physical energy body towards physical work and perseverance. Onyx is great at reclaiming any vitality that has been taken away from the physical energy body by other forces such as stress, tension or worry.

Onyx is a great stone to use if you are putting off physical exercise. Half the time, what stops us from physical exercise is the fear that we won't have the strength to persevere through it. Onyx reclaims your vitality from the fear, so that you go for it, do your best and feel great. Mind over matter. Onyx is the stone of discipline, focus and dedication.

Onyx can be very invigorating overall for the physical energy body, so it is good to have on hand if ever you need a little pick-me-up. If you have arranged to go out somewhere for the evening but are feeling a little tired, onyx can perk you up to face the night, and you never know, you might just end up on the dance floor all night, with onyx in your pocket.

Onyx is not only good for physical strength, it is also good for mental strength. So much of our mental attitude is shaped by the way we carry our body. Onyx gives your physical energy body an upright stance of focus and determination. This can have a great effect on your mental attitude, as it can mirror those qualities in your mental energy body, strengthening your mental determination and power of will. All things start with your physiology.

This makes onyx a great stone to use when the going gets tough with your work or a project, and you need that extra bit of willpower and strength to plough through to the finish line. Perseverance is often the difference between winners and wasted potential. The underdog with physical strength and mental determination can outdo someone with all the talent in the world if that can't push through.

Onyx will give you the strength and willpower you need for whatever it is you want to achieve. It is the Rocky Balboa of the crystal kingdom.

**Qualities:** Strength, determination, willpower, discipline, perseverance.

**Good for:** Physical training and fitness, motivation, pushing through to the finish line of big projects or long-distance runs, competitive sports.

**Issues:** Muscle injuries and strains, feeling tired or weak in the body.

**Mantra:** I am strong in my body and mind. I can do anything.

# Relaxing

## SMOKY QUARTZ

Smoky quartz says RELAX. Smoky quartz works on clearing your physical body's energy field. Like a warm bath after a long day, smoky quartz releases all the stress and tension of the day, helping you to unwind and relax in your skin.

Smoky quartz works wonders on stress-related aches and pains, or stiff necks after a long day at a computer screen.

It is the master stone at stress relief, as it releases the influence of any fear-based narratives that may be a contributing factor to high levels of stress. Smoky quartz releases unhealthy pressures or expectations we have placed on our self, helping us to reclaim our power, find our calm centre and see the situation more clearly.

Usually stress has a deeper message for us. Listen to your soul, calling you to relax! Let smoky quartz absorb all the negative influences that are keeping your body uptight when it is time for rest and renewal. There is nothing to prove.

Where we are all het up in the thoughts and feelings in our heads, smoky quartz grounds us back in our being and transmutes the negative resonances that were transmitted by the pressure of our stressful thinking.

Smoky quartz is a powerful master stone at clearing negative energy, including the negative energy of stressful relationships or environments.

Smoky quartz can be an essential tool if we have had a hard

day at work or a busy day of interacting with lots of energies and people in the hustle and bustle of day-to-day life. It can clear any lingering stressful energies that we have picked up, allowing our body to relax and release the tension of carrying them.

Stress can also be caused by difficult relationships and tense situations. Who has pissed you off today? Let smoky quartz clear your body of their influence over your mood.

Instead of a glass of wine to unwind in the evening, try meditating with two pieces of smoky quartz, one in each hand, and journal the effects it has on you. Notice its effects on the tension in your body, the weight in your mind, and your thought processes regarding the situation you are stressed about.

**Qualities:** Relaxing, unwinding, self-care.
**Good for:** Clearing negative energy, transmuting stressful situations or relationships, self-care.
**Issues:** Stress, bodily tension.
**Mantra:** I am relaxed and stress-free.

# Security and Stability

## TIGER'S EYE

Tiger's eye is a powerful stone with a beautifully soft and comforting energy.

Tiger's eye activates the relationship between the root chakra and the solar plexus chakra. This supports you to apply your power to establish stability in your home life and career. Security and stability is one of our most basic human needs.

Without stability and security, we remain in fight-or-flight survival mode, which makes it difficult for us to progress in our development. Security and stability are one of our most basic human needs, to be able to grow and actualise our power and potential.

Whatever stability and security is for you, tiger's eye will gently steer you in the right direction to achieve that balance.

If you are facing financial difficulty, feeling stuck in your career or facing insecurity in your home life, tiger's eye can stimulate the rationality of your solar plexus to direct your power towards actions that will improve your situation.

Tiger's eye will support you to move out of fear-based fight-or-flight anxieties, so that you can think clearly and practically from a position of composure and sovereignty.

Tiger's eye also works on the area just below your heart, bridging a link between your fears of survival in the root chakra, and the compassionate wisdom of the heart in the heart chakra. This link will alleviate your anxieties and give you a balanced perspective, restoring your faith and trust that life will respond to your call for support.

In working on the area just below the heart, which is the meeting point between earthly and spiritual energies in our body, tiger's eye helps you find your centre in the challenges that are faced in the dichotomy of being a spiritual being having a human experience. If you are a very sensitive soul, who relishes in the spiritual but struggles with meeting physical and financial demands of life, tiger's eye is for you. It will help you identify and clear limiting fear-based energies in your Earth element that keep you from manifesting a livelihood. Often sensitive souls can have an inner sense of rejecting of the physical experience, which also forms limiting barriers to them finding physical stability.

Tiger's eye is a stone of finding your centre when life throws you extremes.

It is a great stone to use for key transitions in life; endings, beginnings, unexpected changes or transformations that may or may not present their own challenges. Tiger's eye helps you find balance and wisdom during these times.

At times we can have a turn of unexpected circumstances and face the destruction of things as we know them, throwing us from one extreme of safety to another extreme of insecurity and fear in the unknown. Whether it be a job loss, a change in your housing situation, or the breakdown of a relationship. As scary and painful as it may be at the time, destruction can be a necessary part of the cycle of change and could be the beginning of a new creative phase in your life, bringing you a fresh start and new direction that you didn't know you needed. Tiger's eye will support you during this transition, and help you find the balance in the difficulty. It will allow you to find a space to let go of the old outdated mode of stability, and call in the new.

If you are resistant to change, tiger's eye will give you the support and comfort you need to trust that the flow of new beginnings is for the best and the emerging new phase in your life will be ultimately fulfilling.

Tiger's eye is also a great companion for healing relationships in the home, or at work.

**Qualities:** Security, stability, balance, centredness, rationality, finding the middle way, renewal, financial security, home-life security.

**Good for:** Going from extremes, unexpected major life changes, e.g. break-ups, eviction, job change, job loss. Healing relationships in the home.

**Issues:** Housing issues, feeling stuck in your career, financial difficulties, career instability, fight-or-flight anxiety.

**Mantra:** I bring forth security and stability in my life.

# Purification

## BLACK TOURMALINE

Black tourmaline is a power stone, clearing out toxic energy interferences like a superhero. It has a phenomenal ability to transmute unpleasant energy into neutral energy that can be reused for good.

Black tourmaline makes way for the light of the soul to clear out any interfering energies that are messing with your flow. I.e. toxic energy of other people's stuff that you have taken on in your energy field, or toxic energy you have picked up from media, such as pressures of comparison or pressures of not being good enough, that have hijacked your mood, motivation and self-esteem.

We are often vulnerable to picking up toxic energy from people or environments or society. Toxic energy can take the form of ideas, entities, addictions, energy remnants from events that have happened in a place or environment, or energy daggers thrown your way from people you are in a toxic relationship with.

Toxic relationships are common and breed an energy dynamic of psychic warfare, where one party or both parties are throwing energetic darts at the other, either in a passive way such as unsaid words but gestures loaded with belittlement, spite, resentment or disdain. Or in an active way of aggressive and unkind spoken words, behaviours or acts of physical violence. The toxic energy of other people that they have projected on to you can stay with you, and really affect your self-esteem, mood and confidence, leaving you feeling heavy and not yourself.

If you have experienced a toxic relationship, and you feel energy remnants of that relationship still alive in your body, working consistently with black tourmaline will cleanse you of all the crap that doesn't belong to you.

It's important to recognise when we have picked up interference because it can be very subtle and can come from anywhere. The best thing to do is to notice how relationships make you feel. Not just relationships with people, but relationships with anything of significance in your life. Your relationship with TV, social media, food, drink, alcohol, work. Notice and pay attention: how does this relationship make me feel? Does this relationship deplete me of energy, does this relationship make me feel good, does this relationship nurture my soul dream? If the answer is no, no, no, chances are this relationship has some kind of toxic anchor in you that it is time to clear.

If there is someone you would like to cut ties with, i.e. someone who you had an entangled relationship with, that although you have parted, their energy still lingers with you, black tourmaline can help you transmute all the energetic anchors you still carry for this person, so that their energy is no longer able to hook on to your field. Programme the black tourmaline to cut the energy cords that still bind you to this person, by removing all the hooks and anchors.

This process can work with things as well as people. For example, if you want to cut ties with an addiction or an unhealthy attachment that has influence over you.

Black tourmaline is great for protection too. If you know you are going to go into a situation where you sense there may be unpleasant energy, take some black tourmaline with you to carry about your person, and programme it to protect you from any psychic daggers or any 'off' energy that is incongruent to your soul dream.

Tourmaline is of good use to protect your energy from anyone who you feel carries an undesirable energy or a strange presence. Or anyone who makes you feel uncomfortable, or anyone who you sense jealousy from. I.e. for all the haters.

In terms of environments, if you spend time in a work or home environment that carries a lot of stress, pressure or aggression, placing black tourmaline in key points in your space can protect you from absorbing that energy.

I recommend black tourmaline to everyone. Black tourmaline is like a ten-day detox in a botanical spa, purifying you deeply of any heavy nasty energy that is in the way of your lightness.

**Qualities:** Purification, protection, clearing out undesirable energy interferences, detoxifying.

**Good for:** Ending toxic relationships, cord cutting, releasing addictions, protection in toxic environments/situations, detoxing.

**Issues:** Energy interferences, feeling congested and heavy, toxic relationships, unhealthy stress from external pressure.

**Mantra:** I purify myself of any interfering energy that does not belong to me.

# Courage

## BLOODSTONE

Survival of the fittest: the mantra underlying the evolutionary impulse of much of life. What does it take to be at our fittest, our strongest and our bravest to face harsh challenges in life? It takes courage. Courage is the strength of our spirit. It resides in our bones, and we awaken it in times that command us to be a warrior.

Whether it's to face a fear, climb a mountain or get through difficult circumstances, our courage will see us through to be a champion of our experience. And if we need a little help, bloodstone will awaken that warrior part of us.

If you are facing a situation where you feel you need support and the heart of a warrior, bloodstone will call on the courage in your bones. It is a stone of evolution and awakens the support of your ancestors, who have laid the path for you.

The wisdom of your lineage is alive in your body, supporting you like the ground below. To be courageous is to live in the intelligence of our body, guided by the visceral instincts that are alive in our blood and the cellular memories of the struggles that our ancestors overcame. What they overcame is what you conquer, what they didn't overcome is what you can change in this life, for them and for you, and together you are stronger in your depth of experience and evolutionary wisdom. Our ancestors are our spiritual allies, and they stand behind us like an army in a long line when we need their strength. They encircle us in infinite circles when we need healing. They stand in front of us to protect us from bad decisions that will dishonour the evolutionary path that they have lived, and that we can continue.

Bloodstone awakens these instinctual realms of the body where our ancestors reside, giving us the courage to face any challenge as an opportunity for growth, feeling our entourage of ancestors supporting us in every step we walk on this earth as a foundation for our own evolutionary impulse.

Bloodstone amplifies the part of you that remembers your connection to the infinite lineage of your bloodline, all the way back to the earliest moments of manifest life. With this connection deep in your bones, you will find a physical strength and courage that is infinite. You can call on this support at any time of need.

To be connected to the spirit of your ancestral line is to be connected to the spirit of your body and its innate wisdom; wisdom that is primal yet deeply spiritual and connected to the earth. Bloodstone carries the energy signature of the blood of the earth, the blood of the rocks, the dirt, the desert, the grasslands, the forests and the ice. Bloodstone not only allows you to call on your ancestors, but it allows you to call on the spirit of the land, the trees, the lofty mountains and other great bodies of strength in the earth's layers that can join you on your campaign to overcome. Bloodstone is the stone of earth memories, and its memories stir your own earthly wisdom, so that you will know what to do in any challenging situation that requires you to be brave.

If you notice patterns to do with health, lifestyles or relation-ships in your immediate family bloodline, meditate with blood-stone on these issues to see if you can get insight into what the root cause is and what you can do in your life to overcome this ancestral pattern for your family.

Ancient peoples across the world have engaged in tradi-tions of paying homage and respect to their ancestors, giving thanks for the path that they have laid and the lives they have made. Not as beings that have long since passed, but as beings that are alive in the blood of the land and the blood of our being. If you want to add a new dimension of support in your life and call on the power of your ancestors, having a ceremony with bloodstone is a good place to start.

**Qualities:** Courage, ancestral healing, strength, evolution.
**Good for:** Honouring and calling on support of ancestors, calling on support from Mother Earth, facing difficult situations where you need strength or bravery.
**Issues:** Family patterns, chronic misfortune, difficult physical circumstances.
**Mantra:** I am a child of this earth, and on my journey. I call on my earth family of my ancestral bloodline. I call on the spirits of the mountains and trees and Mother Earth's layers to give me courage to face challenges so that I may overcome difficulties and evolve.

# 5

# Water

*I express my emotions and listen to my intuition,*
*to come into wisdom, growth and change.*

Earth element is the order of form and our groundedness in it, Water is the fluidity of our inner experience in our relationship to the physical experience.

Water element represents the waves of energies and frequencies flowing through our being all the time, giving rise to our emotions and sensory experience – from the frequencies of pleasure to pain, from joy to sadness, from love to hate. The spectrum of energetic frequencies transmitted in us provides us with a sensory response to process the polarities of life, so that we can become whole.

Just as all rivers can be traced back to the sea, all these energies and frequencies flow from one source; they arise from the infinite, latent, raw potentiality of our unconscious. Our unconscious is the sea. It is our depth. It is the unknown that lies beneath our conscious awareness and the immediate train of thought that we identify as 'I'. The unconscious holds all the hidden and unexpressed parts of our self, yet to be revealed, manifested and experienced. It is the seat of our emotions, our dreams, our imagination, our intuition and creative power.

Mastery of the Water element means listening to these hidden parts of ourselves, as and when they seek to bubble over into our conscious experience. It means expressing them consciously and bringing them into the manifest world, so that we can give birth to ourselves and grow.

Our unconscious is associated with the Great Mother and the Divine Feminine; the invisible mysteries and the unseen potential outside of and before the manifest world, that bring us into being. She is our creative source of inspiration as she moves the energy of dreams and ideas through us from the potent realms within, from which they flow.

## AREA OF LIFE

Water element allows us to enjoy the sensory experience of being a human being in our relationships with our self and in our relationship with others in the world. We are equipped with the energy of emotion as a valid response to process the duality of life.

Emotions are our first language, and in fact the most primal language of the human experience. As a newborn, it is the raw instinctual act of emoting that allows our most basic needs to be communicated and met.

Emotions are our interface with the intelligence of the soul and are our vehicle for learning for survival, growth and change.

They are essentially a measure of the degree to which our physical experience is meeting the needs of our body and soul.

At this primary level, to follow our emotions is to be true to our soul. It is our fear, love, happiness, sadness and anger that can guide and protect us on our soul's journey on earth as a human being, and in our healthiest relationship with our emotions, they can help to lead us to manifesting our soul dream and the wholeness of our true self.

But somewhere along the line, we fall out of a balanced relationship with our emotions, because no one has ever taught us how to be true to this part of ourselves.

We learn from our external environment to suppress, reject, conceal or mask emotions to protect ourselves from our own vulnerability. We avoid emotional expression in fear that we won't be able to cope with the discomfort of our pain or the discomfort of confrontation. We learn that 'Don't be so emotional' is a gold standard by which we must live, to be accepted, through the patriarchal lens of what it is to be a rational, well-functioning human being. We don't want to disturb others or ourselves with our stuff.

It is not just the 'uncomfortable' emotions and sensations we cut ourselves off from. We learn to deprive ourselves of positive emotions and sensory pleasures through repressing natural needs. Out of guilt and the work-life expectations we place on ourselves, we deprive ourselves of the ecstasy of our most basic needs, to rest well, to eat well, to breathe well, to have movement and to have love in our life.

We repress our divine sexuality with the cultural energy of shame or we edit or abuse our sexual expression to meet the commodified patriarchal standards of what it is to be 'sexy'.

Sexual energy is life force itself. It gives frequency to the highest level of intimacy and the divine union of principles. It is the energy of the creative force that pulsates through all of life. To edit it or repress it is to disrupt and deprive ourselves of the true magic of this force.

Emotions and sensory experience enable us to soulfully relate, empathise and be humane to ourselves and each other. To suppress or edit our emotions and sensory experience is to suppress a part of ourselves. It disrupts our relationship with the most human part of being.

The word emotion comes from the Latin verb 'emovere', which literally means to move out; the true process for emotion is for it to *move out* of our unconscious into our conscious expression, where it can be moved out of our body and resolved into a new experience. This processes the depth of our evolutionary path and has a healing effect on the body.

If we do not honour the *moving out* part of the process, by sitting on our emotions, then we disrupt our Water element, causing energetic blockages and disharmony in our energy field. We become damp or, worse still, frozen like ice. With no outward flow and nowhere to express its fluidity, our Water element becomes stagnant and toxic, and we risk becoming stunted in our emotional maturity and growth.

Having trapped emotions that we have unconsciously suppressed means that unprocessed life experiences are in our body, keeping us neurologically and biologically trapped in the past; and while we think we're okay, as we have put a cork on letting our emotions out, masking them with external plasters, the intelligent life force of emotion seeks its way out at any opportunity. We may become constantly triggered by the world, leading to unpredictable, volatile or passive emotional reactions. If we do not give our primary emotions a channel, they can become toxic and leak out in other ways that will ultimately lead to more tension, hurt and chronic pain. This is why sometimes someone's emotional reaction can seem out of proportion to what is actually happening. The actual trigger is from an old unresolved emotion, rather than a response to the situation at hand.

Suppressing or sitting on emotions is not always a conscious decision, it is just something we learn to do. Crystals of the Water element give us the gentle space to be true to this part of our being; to unlock the wisdom in our tension, to resolve old wounds and patterns, to step fully into who we are and find peace in our heart.

## NOURSHING THE VITALITY OF OUR EMOTIONAL ENERGY BODY

Caring for our Water element requires us to take responsibility for our emotions and own the integrity of that process, rather than projecting it on to other people in imbalanced energy exchanges. It means taking care of our response to the world as much as we can; following the signals of tension that indicate that an emotion is trying to come through; following our intuition to read the signs on our soul path; being gentle with ourselves, enquiring how we feel, giving ourselves the space to feel and the space to express. Having relationships where that dimension of ourselves can be nurtured and held. It means maintaining the integrity of the emotional energy body while relating with others; without losing parts of ourselves in the exchange. Emotional relating requires us to own and express our feelings and be in congruence to the emotions, so that we can learn and grow. Otherwise we risk emotions turning toxic, and instead of using emotional energy for expansion, growth and healing and for fulfilling our soul dream, the toxicity of emotion leads us to contract into separation and engage in psychic emotional warfare as a means of controlling or undermining people to protect our self from our own emotional pain. This is a poor use of our energy and only causes and more pain.

Our emotions are not meant to be used for warfare or harm through projection; they are meant to be used for growth and change through expression. On the spectrum of emotion, the more toxic we allow them to become, the more they lead to separation.

**Love Awe Ecstasy Happiness Sadness/Grief Fear Anger Sha**

←————————————————————————————————

**LOVE**

**ONENESS**

All emotions have their place on our path, helping us process the polarity of experience, even the difficult ones.

The energy we have to be most responsible for is our anger. Anger is perhaps one of the most potent forms of energy. It has its place, but when it is misused, misdirected or projected on to others, it can have very damaging effects. The true role of anger is to bring about the change that is needed in our lives. Our journey requires us to learn to transmute anger by unlocking the wisdom behind it to bring about the change it is asking for. But when we do not properly respond to anger, or properly process it by taking responsibility for making changes in our lives, anger will stay in us and become toxic, and that toxicity will emanate into our energy field. We pollute the room and our relationships with it.

We all have anger, it is a healthy emotion; but like all emotions, it needs a healthy outlet. If we don't give emotions a healthy channel through which they can be expressed, they will find a channel for us and they will leak out in other toxic ways.

Guilt Rejection Disappointment Resentment Intolerance Hate

$$\longrightarrow$$

**HATE**

**TOXIC SEPARATION**

Even jealousy can give us insight when we don't suppress it. In its rawest state, jealousy is just the recognition of an aspect in someone that our soul dream would like to manifest in us. But if jealousy is left to go toxic, it leans towards the spectrum of hatred and spite.

Healing toxic emotions involves attending to the original wound, and its primary emotion before it went toxic. What were our needs at the point of vulnerability? And what can we do to attend to that now? What does this part of us need for healing and resolution and closure?

## SYMPTOMS OF WATER ELEMENT IMBALANCES

The main symptom of Water element imbalance is the experience of toxic emotions, causing blockages and robbing us of consciousness and presence. There are many ways in which unprocessed life experiences become toxic and cause blockages in our energy field. For example:

Passive-aggression, irritability or volatile outbursts can result from unexpressed anger.

Post-traumatic stress can result from unprocessed shock or trauma.

Depression can result from unprocessed childhood wounds or unexpressed pleasures of the soul life.

Resentment can result from unexpressed disappointment, neglect or rejection.

Irritability, intolerance and emotional imbalance can

result from unprocessed sadness or grief.
Jealousy or envy can result from unprocessed soul
dreams.

Emotional energy body loss from unprocessed trauma (where we lost a part of our emotional body as a means of survival) can also lead to a feeling of being disembodied.

Emotional energy body loss from a toxic relationship can lead to the feeling that the other person is consuming a part of our minds and emotional body, and we can't shake them off. Life patterns of being in emotionally draining relationships can also be a symptom of imbalances in the emotional energy body.

Emotional energy body loss from an unexpressed wound can lead to an addiction to stimulants.

A feeling of emotional tension or a feeling of being over-whelmed is often a symptom of emergent wisdom from our soul coming through and rubbing up against and conflicting with a facet of our identity that may be unconsciously resistant to emotional change.

## WATER ELEMENT IN OUR LIVES

**Energy body:** Emotional energy body.

**Element qualities:** Emotions, expression, sensuality, sensory pleasure and ecstasy, intuition, inspiration, change, growth and transformation, empathy, Divine Feminine.

**Areas of our life:** Intimate relationships and balanced enjoyment of the senses.

**Relationships:** With others and ourselves.

**Chakras:** Sacral (2nd), Throat (5th).

**Physical body areas:** Lower abdomen, sexual organs, throat, the unconscious.

**Energy body vitality needs:** Expression of emotions.

**Energy body vitality loss causes:** Suppressing or sitting on emotions, stuck, unexpressed or unprocessed emotions, repressed desires, trauma or shock, toxic relationships, emotional manipulation, entanglement, psychic warfare.

**Energy imbalance symptoms:**

*Underactive Water*: Passive-aggression, irritability, projection of or misdirecting emotions at others, resentment, depression, feeling absent, numb, surreal or displaced, losing our self in a relationship, overly sensitive, easily triggered, erratic, cold or frigid, post-traumatic stress, anxiety, self-harm, feeling lost in another person, life patterns of emotionally draining relationships.

*Overactive Water:* Addiction to sensory pleasures, lost in emotions.

## EXERCISE 8: CHECKING IN

Having read about Water element, check in with yourself and see what resonated for you. On a scale of one to ten, rate how fulfilled and balanced you feel in your Water element. Reflect on questions such as:

How in touch are you with your emotions and intuition?

Are you true to your emotions? Do you express them or let them go stagnant and toxic?

Or do you feel your emotions are out of control?

What support do you need to express, balance, or be true to your emotions?

Note down your reflections here:

# EXERCISE 9: RECLAIMING VITALITY OF OUR EMOTIONAL ENERGY BODY

## EXERCISE 9A: VITALITY LOSS AND HEALING ORIGINAL WOUND

Did you recognise any emotional imbalance symptoms in your life? What might be the energetic root causes of these symptoms? Use the descriptions in the 'energy body vitality loss causes' to help you understand where you lose energy or pick up energy blockages. Journal what resonates in the grid below, write freely.

| ELEMENT | Energy imbalance symptoms and life patterns | Causes |
|---|---|---|
| **WATER** Emotional energy body | | |

In holistic healing we address the root cause of the symptom, rather than the symptom itself, so that we can have a true healing and transformation. Once you have identified causes, check in with the wounded part of you, go back in time to when this part of you was originally wounded, the vulnerable part of you, rather than any toxicity. Ask yourself what this wounded part of you needs to have resolution. Choose a crystal from the Compass that will support you with healing that part of yourself.

| What does this original wounded part of me need to have peace and resolution? | Crystal for healing to reclaim yourself |
|---|---|
| | |

## EXERCISE 9B: EXTERNAL RELATIONSHIP AUDIT

List all the emotional relationships you have in the world. It doesn't just have to be with people, it can be with anything you have a relationship with, including work, food, drink, social media etc. Ensure you list all the significant relationships of your life, even if on the surface you think they are without issues. Include teachers, parents, colleagues and friends, lovers – whoever has an impact on your world. The key is to find out whether this relationship drains you of energy or nourishes you with energy. Does this relationship serve your soul dream? Let your intuition guide you to answering.

In this exercise, we can own our role in the relationship. What role have you energetically contracted yourself to play in this relationship? E.g. are you the caretaker? The listener? The addict? The taker? What role do you play? Is this role nourishing or serving an unresolved wound? In this relationship, are you operating from the fear-based self or from a position of wholeness? Start there, without blame or judgement, just with the gentle act of noticing and witnessing. Start with you. All change begins with our bringing awareness to the role we are playing in our life.

If you find a relationship drains you and does not serve your soul dream, then something may need to be resolved – either the nature of the relationship needs to change, starting with you and how you may lose your self in the relationship, or sometimes it may just be time to walk away. If the relationship isn't serving you, it doesn't mean that thing or person is 'bad', it just means that your relationship with it needs refinement.

For any relationship that requires attention, choose a crystal from the Compass to do an insight meditation to bring resolution to this relationship. A quartz, Botswana agate or amazonite are all good stones for an insight meditation, but trust your intuition and choose a crystal from any Element that may be more specific to the relationship. In your meditation with the crystal, ask for insight into how this relationship can become balanced and what action you can take, both internally and externally, to reclaim yourself and find resolution. What are your emotions saying? Then you can choose other crystals from the Compass to help you on that journey. The exercise has been filled in with example entries to give you an idea.

| Relationship | Nourishes energy? | Depletes energy? | Serves soul dream? | Fear-based self relationship or wholeness relationship? |
|---|---|---|---|---|
| Mary | X | | Yes. | Wholeness. |
| Donald | X | | Yes. | Wholeness. |
| Craig | | X | Yes, but ... | Fear-based self. |
| Social media | | X | No. | Fear-based self. |
| Leanne | | X | No. | Fear-based self. |
| Job | | X | No. | Fear-based self. |

| Crystal insight meditation resolution: How can this relationship become more balanced? How might I reclaim myself both internally and externally? What actions do I need to take? | Which other crystals from the Compass might support you on your healing journey? |
| --- | --- |
| | |
| | |
| Craig loves me, but I put his needs before mine too often out of obligation, and it drains me. I want to learn how to be more true to my needs, so I can relate from a place of wholeness. | Amazonite |
| I spend too much time on it out of boredom and end up feeling bad about myself from comparing myself to others. I will address my triggers of boredom by finding more joy in life and refine my relationship with social media to connect with the people and things I love, relating from a place of wholeness. | Chalcedony |
| Leanne doesn't care about me and only wants to talk about herself. I have to walk away. | Amazonite |
| I hate my job. I must find something new and follow my bliss, but I don't know what that is yet. | Chrysocolla |

# EXERCISE 9C: WATER SELF-CARE
# NOURISHMENT AUDIT

|  | **AUDIT** |
|---|---|
| **Self-nurturing and self-care** | How much do you nurture your emotional body? Do you have a safe space to express your emotions? What is your relationship to your emotions? (1–10) |
| **Presence** | How present are you in your emotional body? (1–10) Do you feel emotionally numb? Disconnected? Not all present? |

## CRYSTAL RESOLUTION

What crystals can help me nurture more space for honouring my emotional process?

Use an opal and hematite stone in each hand in a meditation to reflect on what part of your emotional body is absent from your body. Ask when and why it left. Ask the light of the soul to be expressed to reveal what lessons need to come through, to invite this part of you back into your body. Ask the hematite to amplify your call and ground that part of you back in your body.

# Intuition

## MOONSTONE

Moonstone is like the Great Mother; she moves the unchartered waters of your unconscious, the fertile plains of secret knowledge of mysteries and dreams.

Wolves and shamans know the language she speaks. Moonstone is the goddess stone of intuition, the keeper of the mysteries, the link between you, the unconscious mind, and the vastness beyond. Like a high priestess behind the veil, moonstone holds secret access to the deeper realms of the inner self, and sits with the key at the gates of your unconscious. A world that can only be touched by your intuition and the symbols and omens arising in your dreams.

Moonstone invites you into her rainbow cave to taste the mysterious nature of the inner life. She supports you in meeting with the Great Mother who resides near the underbelly of your unconscious, the meeting point between your consciousness and the unborn unified consciousness of creation. Moonstone will lovingly nurture you and keep you safe on a journey of self-discovery and magical illumination. She will help you deepen your trust in the language of your intuition and make the decisions that will keep you on your path. Moonstone deepens you in a wisdom that is beyond the comprehension of the mind, but is a deep inner knowing of the heart.

If you are embarking on a spiritual journey of inner work and seeking to unlock the power of your intuition, moonstone is your ally and a sacred channel.

If you are feeling blocked intuitively or are having trouble trusting your intuition, moonstone will help you restore this relationship so that you listen to your inner voice. If you experience a lot of self-doubt this could be indicative that something is blocking your intuitive capacities and sense of inner knowing. Moonstone will clear any barriers blocking you from being in tune. Sleeping with moonstone under your pillow can also be powerful in helping you understand and remember your dreams. It may also give you some very vivid dreaming, as it amplifies emergent parts of your unconscious self that are trying to be realised in the manifest world.

If you are feeling frustrated by a period of uncertainty, moonstone can give you a sense of patience, and an inner calm that is respectful of the mysteries and cycles of life that are beyond our control. Sometimes we have to surrender the force of our will, and trust that whatever is not flowing is not meant to be. Our time will come. Meditating with moonstone can give you deeper insight into the situation.

Moonstone is a power stone of the Feminine Principle. We are often taught to suppress our feminine side and favour the Masculine Principle of order, reason, rationality. Moonstone can heal your relationship with the Divine Feminine, so you can also honour your inner life, your intuitive powers, and grow.

Moonstone unlocks the fertile mind of pure potentiality, so is a great stone to give you some magical inspiration, if you have spent too much time in the rigid day-to-day structure of the mundane. Moonstone can have your imagination kissed by the Great Mother, to inspire free-flowing creative expression from an unknown magical place.

**Qualities:** Intuition, the unconscious, the mysteries, deep wisdom and rich inner life, patience, calm, imagination.

**Good for:** Inner work, understanding the spiritual nature of reality, healing the Divine Feminine, slowing down, understanding dreams, regulating the menstrual cycle, inspiration for free-flowing creative expression.

**Issues:** Too logical, blocked intuition, frustration about things not going 'your way', self-doubt.

**Mantra:** I trust my being and listen to my inner voice.

# MOONSTONE CREATIVE EXERCISE: DEEPENING YOUR INTUITION AND SPEAKING TO THE GREAT MOTHER

Choose a medium of expression, such as free writing, poetry, drawing or movement.

Spend a few moments of meditation with a moonstone, preferably on a full moon. A full moon is the perfect time in the lunar calendar to express the unexpressed and the fullness of your unconscious self.

In your meditation empty yourself of thoughts and let the waves of the moonstone fill your being. Allow your body to lead the experience rather than the mind. Ask to be at the threshold of the rainbow cave and be a channel for what the moonstone unlocks in you. When you feel ready use your medium to freely express from this deep intuitive place in you. Make an intention to express the strange and unusual. The language of intuition is non-linear, often non-sensical, but makes sense in another dimension of symbols, myths and dreams. To unlock this dimension in you, makes more room for communication with your inner spiritual realms that are guiding you all the time.

# Inspiration

## CHRYSOCOLLA

Chrysocolla injects the sacred back into your life and inspires you with magic.

It commands a spiritual confidence that emanates from the heart. It nourishes a fertile mind, a rich inner life and a spiritual connection to the whole, allowing you not only to be deeply inspired, but also to be an inspiration to others.

Chrysocolla aligns all the chakras in your body so you can become a channel for divine inspiration. It is a Divine Feminine stone; it awakens a goddess energy into your being, the muse from which inspiration flows. Chrysocolla helps you remember that you have your own inner goddess. Whether you are male or female, your inner goddess inspires a relationship of self-love and confidence of the divine feminine. Part of our healing journey is the marriage of the Divine Masculine and the Divine Feminine within. These are spiritual qualities and polarities in all of us that transcend outmoded gender roles.

Remembering our own goddess nature can empower us to recognise our unique contribution to the world, commanding a deep yet humble level of self-respect, helping us to feel at peace and in our power about who we are. It encourages us to take deep care of the richness of our inner world and the inspiration that unfolds when we are in tune with that.

Chrysocolla helps us to express our self from that inspired

place. To be inspired sometimes means being embodied and connected to the great seas of life of which we are just a stream. Chrysocolla reminds us of our connection to the great seas that feed our soul, and increases our fluidity so that we may receive more inspiration and be a vehicle of its flow.

Chrysocolla activates the throat chakra so that we can give words to what is deep and meaningful for us. It helps us name the sacred with the power of our voice, whether it be through a few words, poetry or song. Sometimes it is just enough to hold the presence of what we are feeling, but if it is a time to share our gifts through the voice, chrysocolla will clear any interferences to ensure we can express the sacred with power and wisdom.

Chrysocolla can be a good tool for writing, giving presentations or teaching others, as it helps us transmit the power of the whole into what we are saying.

Chrysocolla grounds you in the field of Mother Earth, but connects you to the unified field of everything through the heart; this gives a healing quality to our words and makes them speak to the many. It also has a beautifully balancing effect on our energy field.

Chrysocolla can support you to honour your word, be inspired by it and be true to what you say.

**Qualities:** Inspiration, personal power, self-expression.
**Good for:** Inspiring others through what you do, being true to your word, poetry, writing, singing, speaking from the heart.

**Issues:** Blocked creativity or expression, low confidence in gifts of expression, all talk and no action.

**Mantra:** I am a goddess and express my power from my heart.

# Joy

## CHALCEDONY

Chalcedony is like a dimension of multi-coloured rainbows, raining jelly candy and dancing Care Bears; a trippy kind of joy. Chalcedony takes you to your happy place.

Chalcedony elicits an inner peace, which can transform into states of spiritual joy and ecstasy if we let it. Chalcedony is one of the best feel-good stones. It amplifies the vitality of the emotional energy body and releases us from old emotional ties, so that we can feel the full sensory joy of just being alive.

Meditating with chalcedony changes your frequency to turn that frown upside down. It releases undue stress and tension from the pressures of life, and revives your sensory capacities to revel in transcendent states of peace.

Do you need to enjoy the sensory pleasures of life more?

If you are finding life a little serious, or if you are taking life too seriously, chalcedony can show you the way, and awaken the joy that is waiting to be experienced in your being. It is there on tap; we just need to breathe into it and remember our essence. Meditating with chalcedony enlivens a delight and a carefree enjoyment in living. It is a great stone to carry if you want to invite in new and enjoyable things to do, to have more fun in life.

On occasion our joy can get stolen. Ever feel like something or someone has come along and ruined your vibe? Chalcedony gives you the power to not take on anyone else's undesirable energy. Often we can be taken off centre by stressful environments or people who project their stuff on to us. Chalcedony helps you to shake it off; it balances your emotional energy body, to get rid of anything that is not yours, so that you can reclaim your space and return to your happy centre. Their stuff is not your stuff! Don't let them kill your joy.

Chalcedony is great if you have a habit of worrying or thinking the worst; it eases any overwhelming emotions and stops them from interfering with our thinking. This has a calming effect of helping you to see life more positively and clearly so that you can relieve your mind from heightened fears or unlikely threats.

This also makes chalcedony a good ally for overcoming phobias. It is very soothing on the emotional body, when it is in an overactive state.

Chalcedony is like a helping hand that shifts us back to centre, to see life from a more balanced point of view. A few quiet moments with chalcedony can help us to reclaim our self from the negative outlook that had a hold of us. It broadens our perspective to include a sense of joy and gratitude, so that we can see the light and make life sweet again. Exciting new prospects will come our way with a refreshed and widened perspective.

**Qualities:** Joy, peace, harmony, spiritual ecstasy, gratitude.
**Good for:** Enjoying life more, refreshing your perspective, balancing overactive emotions, releasing yourself from other people's bad vibes.
**Issues:** Worrying, overthinking, phobias.

**Mantra:** I welcome in deeper currents of joy and
transcendent states of peace and ecstasy in my life.

# Calming

## OPAL (COMMON)

Opal is an incredibly gentle stone. When our emotions are intense, sometimes what we need is gentleness.

Opal works on the emotional energy body; it transmits a very gentle and soothing wave, that brings synthesis to high-intensity emotions, harmonising them into a frequency of deeper emotional intelligence.

If you are feeling emotionally overwhelmed or like your nerves have taken over, opal is like a warm hug from that comforting special person who knows how to calm you down and make you feel like you are going to be alright.

Opal helps you find your ground and centre, when you are feeling lost in the storm of anxiety, stress or any state of over-whelm, where you feel like you just can't cope.

Deep breathing with opal can help you find yourself again; it settles the nerves and the storm, so that you can clear your head and see clearly.

Opal is a stone that balances the Water and Earth element, so it can be very grounding when our emotions become over-active. If you find that your emotions have a life of their own and you often jump from one emotion to the next, opal can gently ground the emotional body, to give you more stability and clarity. Opal harmonises conflicting emotions so that you can moderate your frequency to one of healing and finding the 'middle way'.

Opal is a fantastic stone for grounding our spirit back when it has left us in a shock or a trauma. If you suffer from post-traumatic stress or an emotional imbalance where your emotions are easily triggered by the world, carrying opal or wearing it can help you to clear and resolve the emotional wound at the source. Opal communicates with the emotional body to go to the root cause of an issue, perhaps an imprint of an old trauma, or a life event that you may have even forgotten, but your emotional body is still reacting to. Opal soothes the old imprint of the original wound, and invites it to receive the healing attention it needs. Sometimes we don't even know what the old wound is; opal can reveal and heal that old part of us, to help it find the peace and resolution it is looking for.

Wearing or holding opal for long periods of time, and using deep breathing exercises, can be soothing for any chronic emotional issues that are associated with the mind and thoughts, such as stress, manic states or depression. Often unexpressed emotions become displaced in our mental energy body, and can contribute to imbalances in the way we think and feel. Opal corrects the energy distribution of the emotional body and supports us to find channels for our emotional expression that will help us heal.

If you are someone who is hard on yourself and rejects your emotions, opal will reveal your gentle compassionate side, so that you can be true to your vulnerability and healing needs.

Common opal comes in many colours – white, pink, yellow, brown. All assist with emotional healing and have a soothing quality, but each have their own nuances. The emotional body has an intelligence of its own that is beyond words; let your emotional body choose the right colour for you. Trust your intuition. Let the opal teach you.

**Qualities:** Calming, soothing, grounding, centring.

**Good for:** Getting to the root cause of an emotional imbalance, reclaiming emotional energy body after shock or trauma.

**Issues:** Anxiety, feeling emotionally overwhelmed, stress, post-traumatic stress, easily triggered, overactive emotions, being hard on yourself, depression.

**Mantra:** I am gentle on myself and soothe my emotions to find healing.

# Uplifting

## BOTSWANA AGATE

Whether you need a gentle pick-me-up or you are down in the dumps, Botswana agate is a powerful ally to give you the spiritual uplift that you need.

Botswana agate has a very comforting nature that elevates your heart, mind and awareness to higher spiritual realms, promoting feelings of positivity. Botswana agate spiritualises the physical, emotional and mental energy bodies, reminding you that you are connected to Great Spirit and the unconditional love of the universe. It can give you the spiritual insight you need to heal and problem-solve. It also works on the subtle nature of the spiritual energy body, helping you to address the spiritual blockages that are at the root cause of an issue. This can be particularly effective for issues such as depression or deep sadness.

If life is getting you down and you feel stuck in a sad situation that is out of your power to change, Botswana agate can be a very healing stone to work with. It lifts you up to a higher meditative light state, which shifts your mood and helps you to see the light at the end of the tunnel. Botswana agate can help to pull you out of an issue, to avoid the risk of dwelling on it, and give you spiritual insight and support to let go of that which is out of your control. It can help lift a load, and support you in the process of moving on.

Although Botswana agate is a Water element stone, it is said to hold the rays of the sun to bring people out of dark times.

Again, this makes it a great stone for depression, low moods, heartbreak and difficult periods of grieving.

If you have a problem that you feel you can't solve on your own, take it into meditation with Botswana agate and see how you feel about the problem after. Botswana agate stimulates the crown chakra, inviting in the uplifting support of the rest of the universe, and the other dimensions outside time and space, where transcendent wisdom lies.

Botswana agate is also a stone of the sacral chakra, not only working on the emotions but also working on the fertility of both men and women.

**Qualities:** Uplifting, comforting.

**Good for:** Problem-solving, getting to the spiritual root cause of issues.

**Issues:** Depression, low mood, feeling stuck, grief, heartbreak.

**Mantra:** I am uplifted by my relationship with spirit and am refreshed with new perspective to change my world. I follow the spiritual light of my path.

# Stabilising

## PREHNITE

Sometimes when life throws us all over the place, and frazzles our being, the only way we can find our self again is by centring ourselves back in the heart.

Prehnite unlocks your deepest heart wisdom and allows that wisdom to emanate throughout your body, centring you in a heart space where all things are one. This has a unifying effect on your energy field, bringing order to conflicting emotions, to make you feel balanced and whole again.

Prehnite amplifies the electromagnetic field of the heart; it awakens the strong heart, the brave heart, the warrior heart; the heart that sees the unity in all things, the heart that can see the good, the bad, the ups and downs, and can face them all.

Embodying this quality can be very healing, empowering and balancing for your energy bodies and your wellbeing in general. It stabilises your whole being, which can be great for when you are feeling a bit 'all over the place', or lost or confused in overactive emotions or sensations. Prehnite helps you reclaim your self.

If your energy is feeling scattered, chaotic or nervous, prehnite can reground you in the core of your being, helping you to restore harmony so that you can make sense of things from a place of heart-centred wisdom, strength and power.

Prehnite is a stone of spiritual 'knowing' in the heart. It transforms spiritual ideas and concepts into embodied spiritual experiences, where it is a lived experience right down to your bones, rather than a conceptual idea just in your head. The heart is our entry to communication with the spiritual realms of our experience; amplifying the field of our heart can put us in greater communication with higher dimensions of spiritual wisdom.

Prehnite is a good stone for setting goals that are close to our heart. It will allow our desires to be carried forth by the heart's electromagnetic field for the rest of the universe to hear. The universe speaks the language of love and will respond to your call and cooperate with manifesting your heart-centred intentions. Prehnite helps you build trust in the universe and helps you build trust in the power of your heart to show you the way.

In summary, prehnite reclaims your personal power from emotional issues that are destabilising you, and centres you back into the wisdom of the heart, where most of the answers lie.

**Qualities:** Stabilising, balancing, personal power.
**Good for:** Heart-centred goal-setting.
**Issues:** Anxiety, overactive emotions, frustration.
**Mantra:** I am strong, stable and whole in the power of my warrior heart.

# Acceptance

## AVENTURINE

Aventurine gives you a peaceful knowing that life is perfect in all its imperfections.

It surrenders your resistance to what is and your neediness to control life, and allows you to come into peaceful acceptance, so that you can relax into the arms of life and trust where it is taking you. Aventurine is a great stone for centring yourself in your heart and restoring your trust in life. Like prehnite, it is a stone of the heart centre. It unlocks the spiritual capacity of the heart, which is able to see the divine union in all things. A loving peace and calm will come over you when you drop into the heart space and become a compassionate witness to life.

If you are experiencing anxiety or are placing heavy pressures on yourself about how life should work and what you should be doing, aventurine can heal the inner control freak in you, by revealing your inner Buddha. Our inner control freak can keep us uptight and riddled with tension and anxiety about life. Aventurine allows us to let go of our attachments of how we think people or situations should be, and let go of our entitlements of what we think people or situations owe us. Aventurine will help you to let go of your fears about the uncertainties of life, such as fears about sickness, bereavement, turmoil, rejection, loss or any other challenges you feel you are unable to face.

Aventurine allows you to let go of all these fear-based controlling preferences about how you want your life to turn out, and settles you in the place of loving acceptance of things you can't change.

In this space you can breathe out, relieve tension and find some neutrality, that will let you surrender your inner control freak to the divine.

It is actually a relief to remember that you are not in control of life, nor do you need to be, as there is something much greater at work.

All you can do is make decisions that are aligned to your heart, and then trust the rest of life to respond to that.

Being a compassionate witness to life and surrendering to the divine does not mean you become a passive participant in your life. It means you can handle what life throws at you and move forward with positivity and hope.

It means that you are able to accept the challenges of life's ups and downs, roll with the punches, and move through the experience with serenity and grace.

If your mind is working overtime, or your spiritual work has become too heady, aventurine will realign your energy and ground you in the heart, which is the true place for spiritual work. It will help you feel more settled and balanced and you will see things with renewed meaning.

If you are going through a period of grief, Aventurine can hold you in a loving space to help you honour that process, yet move through it with acceptance.

Aventurine helps you love life and move forward in times of adversity with optimism and serenity.

**Qualities:** Serenity, acceptance, optimism, compassion, faith, hope, trust in life.

**Good for:** Seeing difficult situations in a new light.

**Issues:** Inner control freak, anxiety, emotional turmoil, relationship issues, overactive mind, grief.

**Mantra:** I am, my centre is my heart, I make decisions for myself, the rest I leave to the universe, I trust in life.

# Expression

## AMAZONITE

Amazonite helps us get to the bottom of what we are feeling, so we can express it and find the change in our life that it is asking for.

Amazonite emanates a frequency of truth and harmony, so it has the ability to help us align with our wholeness with acceptance and grace. Rather than be concerned about judgement or fear of change, amazonite enables us to speak our truth, feel our truth and understand our truth and be at ease with that, however messy, confrontational or uncomfortable it may be. It is more painful to sit on our truth than to express it and bring about the change our soul is asking for in our lives.

If you are feeling in a low state of mind, and not sure why, try meditating with amazonite. Ask amazonite to help you express what it is you are feeling. Amazonite will infuse a lightness in your being that will assist you to unlock and express the truth of what is arising in you. Once you've expressed something, you'll often feel better, as you have brought more consciousness to the fullness of your being and honoured the process of growth, wisdom and change.

If you have to express your needs or truth to another person in a potentially difficult conversation, amazonite aligns you to the inner light of your soul, allowing you be clear about what it is you need to do or what it is you need to say. It aligns our voice with our heart so we can speak from a space of heart wisdom without blaming, attacking or getting stuck or attached to our emotions. Amazonite facilitates communication from a space of soulful honesty, which can take the edge off it being a defensive confrontation between our egos.

Not expressing our feelings either to our self or others is often a root cause of an imbalance, and can lead to symptoms of physical, emotional or mental tension. If you often feel tension inside or have a feeling that something is bothering you and you don't know what, try carrying amazonite with you for a few weeks, and see what inner transformations arise.

Be gentle and compassionate with yourself. Amazonite will be gentle and compassionate; it will never push through what you can't handle.

If there is a long-term issue you are experiencing, amazonite will help you bring the light of truth into your past, to support with resolving and healing the original wound that is at the root of blocking your expression. Amazonite also promotes artistic and creative expressions that hold a vibration of truth and authenticity.

**Qualities:** Expression, truth.

**Good for:** Difficult conversations around emotions, getting to the bottom of long-term emotional imbalances or blockages, inner work, self-awareness.

**Issues:** Suppressed feelings, low mood, depression, anxiety.

**Mantra:** I am the Truth Seeker, I am aligned to the light of my truth, I listen to all that arises in me and treat it as information from the truth of my soul, as valid responses to my many lives. I walk the path of evolution and change, to express my True Self.

# Forgiveness

## CHRYSOPRASE

Chrysoprase reminds us that the true nature of forgiveness isn't about judging the person who hurt or oppressed us in a hierarchy of who's right and who's wrong.

Chrysoprase says, it's okay to hold a grudge, hey it's natural, but we can only hold it for so long before it starts to become toxic and eat away at our hearts. Do you want your heart eaten away? No, didn't think so; it's not pretty to be riddled with the pain of resentment and be a prisoner of our own wounds. Why let life be defined by what people did to us? People can be so mean, abusive, neglectful or let us down. But it is our responsibility and spiritual opportunity to heal our precious being so that we can evolve from the experience and be free. Life force wants you to evolve and to stretch you into the whole. Life force will offer all its resources to assist your process; all life force asks of you is your conscious awareness, will and power of intention to say

Yes, I want to heal
Yes, I'm ready to let go and be free
Yes, I want to release the burden of my grudge
Yes, I *want* to forgive

Forgiveness is coming into a space of resolution. It means taking care of our heart's pain and asking what soul lessons are available from the things in our life path that we have encountered. Chrysoprase can help take us past any toxicity and take us to the true wound in the heart to ask, what spiritual light does my heart need to move on from this? Sometimes we have to take care of our heart first before we can enter a space of forgiveness.

Time is a great healer, and in time, when we come into acceptance of what has occurred, we will remember our oneness and that we are all human, and we all err.

If there is ever a stone that reminds us of our oneness, it is chrysoprase. She is attuned to the warming nature of Mother Earth. Mother Earth: possibly one of the most forgiving bodies in the universe. Despite our forgetfulness of her needs and our neglect, she still holds us and provides for us, as the giving mother she is. Chrysoprase holds frequencies of the Mother Earth's blue waters, representing both tears of pain and joy; somewhere in the middle we can find forgiveness.

Don't rush the process – forgiveness can be hard, but it is one of the deepest spiritual journeys of transformation. Let life force move your healing journey and carry a chrysoprase with you on the way. All pain seeks resolution and chrysoprase will give your pain opportunity for resolution. If you've fallen out with someone, be mad with them for as long as you need to be, there is a place for anger, but catch your grudge before it gets smelly and toxic. Chrysoprase can give you a helping hand.

Do you need closure to help with your forgiveness and resolution? Meditate with chrysoprase for answers on how to meaningfully do that, from the heart.

I love you, I forgive you, I'm sorry. This is a Hawaiian prayer that is used in healing ceremonies.

Use chrysoprase to look in the mirror and look into your own eyes – see your soul and the soul of all those you love and hate, and recite, I love you, I forgive you, I'm sorry. Extend this to yourself and all those in your life.

Let your heart be free.

I love you, I forgive you, I'm sorry.

**Quality:** Forgiveness, compassion, resolution, spiritual evolution, oneness, reconciliation.

**Good for:** Resolving the past, making up with people you've fallen out with, taking the edge off your grudge so that you can reconcile, letting go.

**Issues:** Resentment, hurt.

**Mantra:** I love you. I forgive you. I'm sorry.

# Emotional Healing

## ARAGONITE (BLUE)

Blue aragonite is one of the most transformative of the Water element stones, and assists in bringing harmony and balance to your emotional energy body. It is a stone of spiritual change, compassion and expansion, and unlocks your ability to grow and evolve from difficult emotions.

Blue aragonite works wonders on your ability to heal from the past. It softly eases emotional attachments to people or to things that have happened to us. Meditating on people or life events that you are finding difficult to let go of using blue aragonite will assist you in coming into a state of peace and harmony, giving you spiritual insight to reclaim yourself, evolve from past hurts and become an expanded version of who you are.

After meditating with blue aragonite, you will often know what it is you need to do to gain closure on an emotional situation from the past.

If you are finding it difficult to move on from emotional pain, and are finding that the pain still defines how you experience the world, spending long periods of time with blue aragonite can be very helpful in giving you compassion for yourself, and a healed emotional perception that will help you to move on.

Blue aragonite is a powerful stone to use in difficult times, where your emotions feel raw or unbearable. It helps you to honour your emotions, while soothing them with the light of your own inner wisdom, which can provide a comforting space from which to move through what you are feeling, knowing that there is light on the other side.

Blue aragonite is great for releasing shock from the body after a trauma. Sometimes parts of our emotional energy body leave us in a shock or trauma so that primal fight-or-flight responses can override our body and protect us in the situation. If we don't release the shock from our body or heal from the trauma of the situation, it may be difficult for that part of our emotional energy body to return, leaving us feeling numb, empty and displaced. Blue aragonite can make us feel whole again, healing the shock from our nervous system, and gently calling to our spirit to come back home into our body.

Blue aragonite is the ultimate stone for emotional healing, soothing your emotional body and helping you to prepare for closure, change and moving on to something new.

**Qualities:** Emotional healing, spiritual evolution.

**Good for:** Healing childhood wounds or traumatic events, learning how to listen to our emotions and grow from them, healing life patterns.

**Issues:** Emotional imbalances, trauma, trouble letting go of the past.

**Mantra:** I process my emotions and find deep wisdom and change.

# 6

# Fire

*I reclaim my power and manifest my soul dream.*

Respect to the great fire of the sun, that brings light, warmth and energy to much of life. Without fire, there is darkness and little life. Fire element represents us lighting our own fire and living life to our fullest. Through fire we take action and inject passion, will and determination into our lives; we apply our minds, to fulfil our potential and shine our light in the world. Through fire we make a change, and we make a difference.

Fire is the alchemy of our will that can bring about transformation in the conscious meeting of spirit and matter. The ingredients of Fire are oxygen (Air), fuel (Earth) and friction. Through our spiritual values of our Air element rubbing with the manifest nature of our Earth element, we manifest our power of will. But playing with fire can be dangerous; it has potential to both create and destroy. In our journey towards truth, we fulfil our Fire element when we use our power *consciously*; from a soulful position of connection, wholeness and service, rather than a fear-based position of separation, deficit and self-centredness.

## AREA OF LIFE

Fire is our ability to exert our personal will in the world to actualise our power and potential. It relates to our mental energy body and our capacity to apply our mind to express our gifts and passions. Fire relates to the management of power and the ability to shape the trajectory of our lives. Power is about living in the sovereignty of the warrior heart. The conscious management of power requires us to assert our self and pursue our vision without caring what others may think; and without compromising the truth of who we are. It may require us to make difficult decisions, or hold our ground in conflict or oppressive environments. Soul power or conscious power isn't the same as ego power. Whereas ego power serves values of separation and personal gain, soul power serves the soul dream, and by virtue serves the whole.

Fire makes us take responsibility for our lives, to apply ourselves, to stand up for ourselves, to believe in ourselves, and not be afraid to express our uniqueness. It is about feeling the fear and doing it anyway. Failure is only another opportunity for evolution and refinement. Fire is not about staying in the safety blanket of familiarity. It is about positive action and transformation and sheer confidence in what we want to acheive in our heart.

## SYMPTOMS OF FIRE ELEMENT IMBALANCES

Low confidence and self-esteem can be both a symptom and a cause of Fire element imbalances, causing us to lose our power to people, society or ideas.

Symptoms of weak fire include:

over-performance, expending our energy outwardly
from a space of insecurity, lack or neediness to prove
ourselves
anxiety
social anxiety or performance anxiety
panic attacks
exhaustion
depletion
suppressing our individuality and editing who we are for
approval, staying a prisoner of other people's ideals

In power loss, the tension between our soul's emergent power and the blockages that resist it can manifest in common symptoms such as:

stress
confusion
indecision
life patterns of toxic relationships where we lose ourself
and our identity

When we have weak Fire element, where our fears or oppressive people get in our way, there can be symptoms of:

inactivity
patterns of giving our power away to others

playing it safe
mind being easily programmed or controlled by others
   or society

When our mental energy body is stagnant and without anything meaningful or soulful to apply its energy to, our unexpressed soul gifts can lead to:

depression
addiction
patterns of behaviour where we avoid applying
   ourselves, e.g. idleness, watching too much TV, idle
   time on the internet or social media
laziness
procrastination

Symptoms of excess fire occur when we are overidentified with our power and are stuck in that level of experience. We can become entitled, arrogant, egotistical and self-centred. Signs of excess fire include:

abusing one's power
taking power from others
moving too quickly
thinking too quickly
'fiery' – easily stepping into conflict with people
saying too much
drunk with ego power

**egotistical**
**arrogant**
**abusive**
**controlling**
**obsessive**
**control freak**
**overactive, doing too much**

If you recognise any of these symptoms of excess fire, it is best to work with crystals of the others elements to counteract this imbalance.

## FIRE ELEMENT IN OUR LIVES

**Energy body:** Mental energy body.

**Element qualities:** Power, will, confidence, passion, actualisation, assertiveness, transformation.

**Areas of our life:** Directing our mental energy to express our individuality, gifts and to fulfil our power and potential in the world.

**Relationships:** Society and the world.

**Chakras:** Solar plexus (3rd).

**Physical body areas:** Rational mind, stomach.

**Energy body vitality needs:** To feel safe and free of harm, to express individuality. To have meaningful things to apply ourselves to.

**Energy body vitality loss causes:** Giving away our power to people, fears or society. Compromising facets of individuality and allowing the external world to shape our identity for acceptance. Over-exerting ourselves, coming from a space of lack. Inactivity coming from a place of fear.

**Energy imbalance symptoms:**

*Underactive Fire:* Indecision, anxiety, panic attacks, mental exhaustion or depletion, stress, confusion, inactive, playing it safe, idleness, procrastination, laziness, depression, addiction.

*Overactive Fire*: Arrogance, egotistical, entitled, abusive, 'fiery' – easily getting into conflict, controlling, oppressive, control freak, obsessive.

## EXERCISE 10: CHECKING IN

Having read about Fire element, check in with yourself and see what resonated for you. On a scale of one to ten, rate how fulfilled and balanced you feel in your Fire element. Reflect on questions such as:

Do you exert your power in the word towards your passion?

Where do you lose power, or give away your power?

Who or what owns you?

Who is winning, you or your fears?

Where do you apply the power of your mind?

Do you feel empowered or powerless?

Where can you reclaim vitality?

Note down your reflections here:

# EXERCISE 11: RECLAIMING VITALITY OF OUR MENTAL ENERGY BODY

Where are you losing your power? These exercises allow us to identify relationships, environments, conditioning or life events that are at the root of an energy blockage or power loss; so we can then choose a crystal to help us reclaim our power.

| ELEMENT | Energy imbalance symptoms and life patterns<br><br>E.g. social anxiety, giving away power in relationships, what energy are you operating from? | Causes<br><br>What is the cause of the symptom or life pattern? E.g. lack of confidence, childhood wound? |
|---|---|---|
| FIRE<br>Mental energy body | | |

## EXERCISE 11A: VITALITY LOSS AND HEALING
## ORIGINAL WOUND

Did you recognise any mental energy vitality loss symptoms in your life? What might be the root causes of these symptoms? Use the descriptions in the 'energy body vitality loss causes' section of the box on page 164 to help you. Note down what resonates in the grid below, write freely. Holistic healing seeks to address the root cause of the symptom, rather than the symptom itself, allowing for a true healing and transformation. Once you have identified causes in your life, choose a crystal from the Compass in the Fire element that will support you to overcome these issues.

| What action can I take to support this part of me? What changes can I make in my environment to support me? | Which crystals from the Compass will help me reclaim my physical vitality? Which crystals from the Compass will help me to overcome life patterns related to Fire element imbalances? |
|---|---|
|  |  |

## EXERCISE 11B: RELATIONSHIP AUDIT

Reflect on every relationship you have in the world. With people, things, habits, behaviours, jobs, groups, society. Get a sense if there is a power imbalance in this relationship. Is there an invisible hierarchy? Do you place someone above or below you? Do the other person's needs, preferences, or opinions

| Relationship | Take power from others? | Give away power? | Serves soul dream? | Fear-based self relationship or wholeness relationship? |
|---|---|---|---|---|
| | | | | |
| | | | | |
| | | | | |
| | | | | |

disproportionately come before yours? Are you giving your power away in the relationship? Are you taking power away in the relationship? Reflect how and do an insight meditation to reclaim your power or heal your need to take power from others. Everything is relationship! Assess if your relationship serves your soul dream and whether it is a fear-based relationship or a wholeness-based relationship. Answer intuitively and freely.

| Crystal insight meditation resolution: What energy am I coming from in this relationship? What is the wound in me that this energy comes from? What part of me needs healing? What soulful part of me needs to come through to restore power balance in this relationship? How might I reclaim my power both internally and externally? What actions do I need to take? | Which other crystals from the Compass might support you on your healing journey? |
| --- | --- |
|  |  |
|  |  |
|  |  |
|  |  |

## EXERCISE 11C: FIRE SELF-CARE NOURISHMENT AUDIT

|  | **AUDIT** |
|---|---|
| **Self-nurturing and self-care** | How much do you nurture your mental energy body with meaningful things to apply yourself to? (1–10) |
|  | How safe and free of harm do you feel to express your power and individuality in your current situations? |
| **Presence** | How present are you in your mental energy body? (1–10) Is your mind consumed with thoughts? |

## CRYSTAL RESOLUTION

What can you do more of to nurture the vitality of your mental energy body? What shifts can be made in your environment so that you can express your gifts fully? Which crystals can support you on that journey?

Use a Fire crystal to reclaim the fullness of your fire!

For overactive fire, try some Air crystals to bring the power of your spiritual awareness to these imbalances and restore presence.

# Motivation

## ORANGE CALCITE

Orange calcite is a fire stone, but it also works on the emotional body to clear emotions that are demotivating your fire.

Orange calcite gives you a clear-out in your sacral chakra of any energies that you are holding on to, that are pulling you down. Old fears that are unexpressed or unresolved will get a clearing and any thoughts about how you can't do it, and how hard it's going to be, will get a slap on the wrist. Orange calcite is playful, so your kick up the bum to get on with things will be with lightness and humour. Orange calcite is effective at clearing emotional blockages, so this can mean that you may experience a period of emotional release, of moaning about how crappy things are and how you want to give up, before reaching a period of 'Oh yeah, I can do this, I want to do this! let's go!' Better out than in is the saying, and sometimes we need to have moan before we realise that our moan is BS; then we can have a laugh at ourselves. Orange calcite makes us see the lightness in things. It lightens the load of the task at hand, reminds us of enjoying the process, and encourages us to just get going with joy and positivity.

Orange calcite injects the passion back into our life, giving us the fuel and playfulness to just make a start. It's a gentle stone so the effects are very gradual, but you will notice a calmness in your heart that lets you breathe, and through exhalation, release your demotivating emotions so that you can get on with things. If you are feeling joyful, orange calcite will resonate with that and amplify it.

Orange calcite is a stone of enjoyment and pleasure, reminding you to enjoy the ride and the sensory experiences of being a human being. The enjoyment factor will disperse the mental dread that you carry about getting started.

Sometimes the sensory experience is what we need to be reconnected with to restore our motivation.

**Qualities:** Motivation, uplifting, pleasure, enjoyment, playfulness.

**Good for:** Healing old emotional experiences still in the body that are in the way of your motivation.

**Issues:** Procrastination, depression, repressed desires, emotional blockages, moodiness, despondency.

**Mantra:** I am motivated by the joy of the journey, so let's begin.

# Determination

## YELLOW CALCITE

Get clear, stand up and move towards your goal. YOU CAN DO IT! Yellow calcite engenders a fierce determination that is clear-headed, confident but also fun.

Your solar plexus chakra is innately linked to the processing power of your rational mind. Yellow calcite strengthens this link, clearing away the cobwebs in your head that are in the way of you directing your power towards the task at hand. Yellow calcite clears the energetic remnants of any distractions that are keeping you from achieving your goal.

Yellow calcite works wonders on the mind. Whatever it is that you need to put your mind to, anything that requires the power for your intellect, yellow calcite will assist you in working on it with clarity, proactivity and ease.

If you are flagging and need a bit of persistence, have yellow calcite on hand to give you an uplifting alignment to get back into a steadfast vibe. If you need to put your mind to a new project or a new life direction that you have been putting off, keeping a yellow calcite on you will keep nudging you in the right direction. If you are letting your fears get in the way with thoughts such as 'I cant do it, I don't have the time, it's not going to work, it's too hard', a few moments of meditation with yellow calcite will knock all those fear-based excuses on the head, neutralising their power over you and redistributing your mental energy on to your goal.

---

Sometimes we need to get very single-minded and bring all our mental energy on a focused point like a laser, to blur everything else out and push on with our task at hand. That is what yellow calcite can do for you.

It is a very solid stone. It doesn't take any prisoners. It will bring out the fierce confident determined warrior in you, but also the one who likes to have fun with it.

Word of warning! If you are already determined, don't use yellow calcite as it may give you a headache, or you may become a little bit overbearing!

**Qualities:** Determination, confidence, persistence, intellect, insight, action, dedication, steadfastness, assertiveness.

**Good for:** Achieving a goal, putting an idea into action, fulfilling a dream, putting your mind to something, starting a new project or life direction.

**Issues:** Easily distracted, lacking discipline or willpower, procrastination, lacking confidence or focus in achieving your dream.

**Mantra:** I am fierce and confident and determined to achieve my goal!

# Action

## CARNELIAN

Whereas the next crystal in the compass, fire agate, stimulates the inner experience of creativity, carnelian stimulates the outer experience of creativity. Carnelian is a stone of embodied movement and inspired action. It is an energising stone that injects playfulness and enjoyment in everything that you do.

If you have some ideas that have not yet been put into action for whatever reason, carnelian stimulates the confidence and vitality to get your body into action. Whereas golden apatite promotes a mental confidence, carnelian releases an instinctual vitality that commands a confidence in the body, helping you to go forth in an unapologetic, playful expression of who you are. Carnelian's body confidence frees you of inhibitions or of reasons why not to do it, and awakens the part of you that just loves to move and get started. If you feel overwhelmed by the sheer idea of doing something, a few moments with carnelian will make you want to dive in. It is a stone of 'enjoying the process'.

Carnelian floods the body with this instinctual vitality, allowing raw activity to flow. If you are someone who gets lost in indecision or procrastination, or who lacks confidence in getting things done, carnelian will inspire you to feel the fear and enjoy doing it anyway. Whatever is the right thing to do, carnelian inspires you to just take action and follow the flow.

Carnelian makes you enjoy the gift of the body and stimulates a desire to put your body to good use. It helps you find the part of you that revels in the experience of 'doing'. This can be great for increasing your productivity and bringing back a little excitement to what it is you're engaged with. If you have a job to do that doesn't inspire you, try using carnelian to help you find the fun in it.

Carnelian is invigorating, as it stirs sexual vitality and awakens dormant energies within. It revitalises the creative, sexual and power centres, giving you a warming lift that travels right through the body. Sexual vitality is not just an energy for the act of sex. It is a sacred life force that can be used for creativity, movement and expression from an inner place of playfulness and divine power. If you are shy about your body or have issues that are repressing your sexuality, carnelian can arouse sensuality and self-love, helping you to feel comfortable in your own skin and enjoy the pleasures of being you. Carnelian will help you embrace your natural sexual nature.

Carnelian may inspire all things fluid, beautiful and expressive, such as dance, exercise, free movement or yoga. It may even inspire you to engage in sensual pleasures of beautifying and pampering the body.

Carnelian is a powerful stone with lasting effects. Try spending a whole day with it and see what happens the next day. It will bring you to life as a sexual being, arouse vitality to get you at your most productive, and invigorate the body from within to stir you into action to achieve your goals. Just do it!

**Qualities:** Action, body confidence, creativity, sexuality, vitality, enjoyment.

**Good for:** Getting started, enjoying the process, exercising, movement.

**Issues:** Procrastination, inactivity, 'all talk and no action', low confidence.

**Mantra:** I enjoy the gift of my body, and honour its gift by taking action.

# Creativity

## FIRE AGATE

Fire agate is an ally of creativity and the creative process. It stirs the cauldron of the creative centre; the sacral chakra. You may even feel it swirl in your belly. It will inspire expression through any medium, and support you to bring your idea to manifestation. Whether it is your greatest masterpiece or simply a new idea for your living room, fire agate brings more vitality to the creative act by stimulating the lower chakras and energising the creative aspects of the physical, emotional and mental energy bodies. If you are facing creativity blocks, keeping fire agate on you can support you in the process.

Fire agate surrenders your mind from the need to control the creative process and lends more energy to the unknown creative forces within. Deep inside, in the unseen intelligence of your unconscious, connections are being made to dream a dream, an idea or an innovation into existence. If your creativity is blocked or not flowing, it may be that there is more dreaming to be dreamt or more experiences to be experienced before it can be brought forth into fruition. The creative process cannot be forced and will arrive when it is cooked and ready. If it's not yet flowing, stop, do something else and trust that something is still looking within.

Fire agate helps to stir the cooking. It amplifies the pulsating creative force inside your creative cauldron, and when you are ready to spill over, fire agate will channel more energy to your

'Aha!' moment and carry you effortlessly in a vibrant outflow of creative expression.

Fire agate gets you out of your head and into an instinctual intelligence, making it easier to surrender your inhibitions, make decisions and take risks. It promotes vitality, sensuality and grounding in the body, making it also a great stone for healing your divine sexuality and your enjoyment of the senses. It awakens the sexuality of your sacral chakra, which may be beneficial for embracing the body and clearing any issues and imbalances in your relationship with intimacy. Fire agate can also promote sexual confidence.

We are creating our lives all the time. Fire agate invites in the magic of the creative force, allowing us to create more magic in our lives.

**Qualities:** Creativity, sexuality.
**Good for:** Artistic projects.
**Issues:** Creativity blocks.
**Mantra:** I am a channel for creativity and through me creativity flows.

# Confidence

## GOLDEN (YELLOW) APATITE

Golden apatite is the stone for aligning your mind and will. It helps you to get clear in your head about what you really want to express in your life, and then gives you the inner confidence and conviction to go out there and express it.

True confidence isn't about boosting the ego; it is about having the clarity of conviction in your own ideas. It is about dispelling the cloud of self-doubt and need for approval that may be causing havoc in our energy field.

It is about talking eloquently about who we are and what we want to do, with unapologetic grace. It is being comfortable in our ideas, and our ability to manifest them. That's confidence.

If you have a work situation that requires you to ooze confidence and charisma, but you're feeling a little low in confidence, golden apatite will give you an added alignment with your soul qualities so that you can shine from within and be a boss at whatever you do. People will be uplifted by your truth, your ideas and your soul congruence. This makes golden apatite great for public speaking or performance.

It can also assist when a life or work situation requires an assertiveness and a powerful eloquence to transmit our truth. If we are shy or have social anxiety, golden apatite can help us to relax and be ourselves.

When our mind is clear about what we want to achieve, and aligned to the power of our will, that is fire! That is the magic

---

formula for creation, and our ability to create from that space cannot be held back by anyone. Golden apatite unlocks this clarity of mind and intention. Ideas will flow and your mind's capacity for problem-solving and organising information will be heightened to make creative leaps and bounds towards manifesting your goal. The universe will respond with happy meetings and opportunities. Success is yours. Go get it!

If we are feeling unclear about what it is we want to do in our lives, and what would best serve our purpose, golden apatite can help us get clear in knowing what we need to do.

Meditating with golden apatite will amplify the innate confidence of your soul's qualities, and the brightness of your fire element will dispel all the energy clouds. You will feel a sense of clarity about what it is you need to do, your mind will become aligned to your will and suddenly you'll find your brain making new connections to make forward motions towards your goal. Solutions will appear to things that seemed like problems before and there will be an eloquent flow to your creative efforts. You'll be able to take the risks and be assertive in achieving your goals.

Go out there and confidently do what you need to do to make your dream come true. Don't be shy about it. Grab your golden apatite and be of service to the world, confidently expressing your true power and potential.

Golden apatite is rarer than other crystals in the Compass. You will find that only small pieces are available but size is no issue, as it packs a punch. Golden apatite is the stone for mental confidence, for body confidence choose carnelian.

**Qualities:** Confidence, assertiveness, clarity of mind, manifestation, success.

**Good for:** Pursuing an idea or dream or business, public speaking or performance, social situations, finding solutions, problem-solving, innovation, creative leaps and flow.

**Issues:** Low confidence, nervousness, self-doubt, procrastination, social anxiety.

**Mantra:** I am a confident expression of me! I am a boss! I am clear and my ideas flow. I know what I need to do to get on with it and make it happen.

# Passion

## ORANGE (SPESSARTITE) GARNET

Orange garnet is a really powerful stone, having an almost immediate effect on your energy field. It is a full-body experience. It emanates a light and warmth in you that feels like the sunshine kissing your face on a balmy day. It awakens and raises the vitality in the sexual, creative and power centres, readying your total body for passionate action.

Orange garnet has an uplifting effect on your mental and emotional energy fields, clearing any heavy stagnant resonances of moods or unconscious thoughts that may be bringing you down and interfering with your fire and creative flow. There are many things that can get in the way of what we love to do. Some of the time it can be external factors or life demands, but most of the time, it is us. Whatever it is that is unconsciously holding you back from your passion or creativity, whether it be fear-based mental scripts, false beliefs, low confidence or self-esteem, orange garnet will release those blockages from you, giving your emotional and mental energy body room to breathe, room to feel whole and room to feel a lust for life.

Orange garnet relights your fire. Whether you want to feel more passion in your work, your creative endeavours or your sex life, orange garnet is the perfect companion. If you are experiencing a low sex drive or want to reinvigorate your sexual relationship, orange garnet works very well at stimulating sexual energy, in a way that surges up through the body, releasing any limiting inhibitions or old wounds. If you have lost a passion in the work you do, and are feeling groggy and tired about it, try using orange garnet to see if it will help reinvigorate your relationship with it; if it doesn't, it may be time to trust your dampened feelings and move on from your work.

Sometimes we can get so bogged down in our emotional and mental energy bodies that we don't have enough emotional or mental vitality to feel engaged in life any more. When the mental and emotional energy bodies are consumed by thoughts and feelings that are no longer serving them, we are deprived of the vitality we need to feel passionate about life. Often we don't know the reason for our lack of passion; only the signs and symptoms of feeling low, tired, lost, unmotivated or uninspired.

Using orange garnet will amplify the more creative, carefree and sensual part of you that responds to life with feeling and direction. When this part of you is awakened, it will make you realise the nature of the old stagnant parts of you that were in the way of that flow, helping you to recognise any old attitudes to life that it may be time to let go of. Orange garnet helps you rediscover what you care about and what lights you on fire.

Orange garnet gets you out of your head and back into your body and your sensory experience of living, so that you can feel the fire and apply yourself to whatever it is you really want to do, feel or achieve.

**Qualities:** Passion, creativity, sexuality, manifestation.

**Good for:** Needing reinvigoration at work, home, in your sex
life.

**Issues:** Unmotivated, uninspired, low sex drive.

**Mantra:** My fire is lit and I feel for life again.

# Leadership

## SUNSTONE

Sunstone gives you permission to shine like the sun, be seen, be heard and be noticed. You have something powerful to share. Own it.

Sunstone's energy descends on you, almost like the sun itself, guiding you to the light of who you are. Sunstone ignites your inner being to shine through, to stand up for your truth and what you believe in. If you have to have a difficult conversation, sunstone can remind you of the authority of your light and help you be assertive from a position of integrity and respect. Sunstone is a good stone to work with when you have to work with a lot of people and get your point across to serve the greater good of the group.

Sunstone lightens your load, helping you to delegate and call on support when you are feeling overwhelmed. Don't be afraid to take a leadership role and direct what needs to happen for a collective goal to be reached. Whether it be at home, at work or any kind of team activity that involves planning, cooperation and action: use your voice to delegate.

Sunstone helps you direct your efforts towards achieving a collective goal, so it is also a good stone for cooperative teamwork.

If you are in a relationship dynamic that is toxic or abusive, sunstone connects you to your light and power, clearing away the influence of the energy attachments to awaken you to the insight 'oh yeah I don't have to put up with this shit'.

If you have been blind to a relationship that is actually diminishing your light, sunstone will highlight what is wrong in the relationship and make you speak up and take action.

If you are shy about stating your needs or are someone that puts others' emotional needs first, sunstone will bring out that neglected part of you that needs to be heard. It is not selfish to state what your needs are; when you shine the light of your truth you are also serving others and the greater good of a situation.

If you are someone who conceals your gifts and plays small for the sake of not offending others, sunstone is for you. You playing small does not serve anyone. The sun doesn't play down or apologise for its brilliance and neither should you. Imagine if it did, what a cold lifeless world we would live in. Show yourself and all your qualities and take a bold step to lead in whatever it is that you want to do in your heart.

**Qualities:** Leadership, assertiveness, teamwork, sharing the light of your soul dream in the world.

**Good for:** Speaking up, delegating, standing up for yourself in toxic relationships/situations, managing people/projects, sharing your talents, owning your power.

**Issues:** Playing small, disempowered, shyness.

**Mantra:** I speak up and I shine!

# Assertiveness

## MALACHITE

Malachite brings out the fiercest version of you. Malachite brings out your inner warrior; the warrior who is ready for whatever comes his or her way, the warrior who no one can mess with, the warrior who will not be swayed from the path of their heart.

The warrior is true to herself and she lives her truth; no one can influence her to be what she is not. The warrior needs no approval. She owns who she is, moves forward to achieve her soul dream and carries herself like a boss. Nobody can stop her, including herself.

We can be our own worst enemy at times; we can give up at the final hurdles when, really, we need to push through. We can back down to bullies when, really, we need to stand up and not take it. We can dim down our inner light to stay safe and not offend anyone when, really, we need to go out there and shine bright like the sun.

Malachite gets your head up and channels the proverbial eye of the tiger with a fierce roar, giving you the strength, vision and assertiveness to plough through and triumph. Backing down or giving up on your truth or your potential is not an option. The awakened warrior in you will slay any thoughts or feelings that seek to demotivate you or put you down. When you are carrying that inner conviction in your heart, it will make it very difficult for others who seek to intimidate or undermine you.

If you have a point to put across and you struggle to be heard by certain individuals, malachite will help you reclaim your power so that you can assert your voice with might.

If you need to step into a difficult situation that will involve confrontation, malachite will channel your inner sovereignty and call on the line of your ancestors to stand behind you like an army, to lift your voice, your power and your presence, so that you can stand your ground and overcome anyone's attempts to steal your power. The warrior is unafraid of confrontation and is always able to protect herself from people or mind influences that want to steer her off track.

Do you know any warriors? What would your life be like if you unleashed this quality in yourself? Do you know the warrior in you? It may be time to bring her forth to stand up for your truth and what you really want in life. You deserve it. If you are afraid to go out there and be assertive in your own individuality, meditate with malachite and meet the warrior who is waiting to come out of you. Let the warrior out, she will rebuild your power and diffuse the fears that stand in your way.

If you face patterns of people-pleasing, malachite is a great stone for helping you to own every facet of who you are un-apologetically. It is okay if people don't like you.

If you are engaging in habits that are sabotaging your soul dream, malachite will help you reclaim your power.

Malachite is the ultimate stone for psychic strength and assertiveness. It illuminates your whole inner being with fire and will, so that you are unwavering in following your heart and soul.

You are a force to be reckoned with if you allow yourself to be! The world is waiting for you to bring forth the power of your soul.

**Qualities:** Assertiveness, psychic strength, psychic protection, fierceness.

**Good for:** Owning your individuality, going for your dreams, handling difficult conversations or imbalanced power dynamics, reclaiming your power.

**Issues:** Bullying, psychic warfare, people-pleasing, self-sabotaging, power loss, low confidence and low self-esteem.

**Mantra:** I reclaim my power. Nothing can stop me. Bring it!

# Prosperity

## CITRINE

Citrine obliterates the illusion of separation between you and the universe, and you and your future goals, and amplifies your intentions and desires for the universe to respond.

You are an extension of the universe and the universe is an extension of you. Every life form pulsates with its own intelligence, powered by the life force that unites them and allows them to work in divine cooperation to manifest balance. What do you want to manifest? When you make a decision that is true in your heart and soul, the universe will cooperate to give you what you need; it will take care of you in its abundance of life. Call it forth. Citrine amplifies your intention. But if there is an ounce of doubt or fear or neediness surrounding your decision, it is merely the fear-based self's imitation of a decision of the heart, and you may just attract more of the same, until you transcend the blockage.

Citrine works with where you are at. If your decision is from the heart, it will bring you that back in abundance. If your decision is from fear, then the universe will respond with supportive lessons and opportunities for you to transcend that fear. Either way it will all eventually get you to the same goal of prosperity.

If you are someone who struggles with finances, citrine is a stone to carry in your wallet, to ensure you always have enough. What false-self narratives about money reside in you that keep you from being comfortable?

Citrine is not about greed, or accumulation of wealth for being wealthy's sake. Citrine is about prosperity and success (as defined by you) in whatever your path is. If you are coming from a place of balance instead of greed or neediness, citrine will be your guiding light. If you are coming from a place of greed and neediness, citrine will simply tell you about yourself, through more life patterns, until you get the picture.

How deserving do you feel of achieving what you want? How much do you believe in what you have set out to achieve? These are the kind of energetic blocks that will be interfering with you manifesting what you want to create in your heart. If these low self-beliefs are there, citrine will help you see them.

And if they are not there, citrine will send your message loud and clear to the rest of Life, *I am ready, I am here, and I am willing to receive.*

The rest is up to you, putting the work in, and following up on your intentions. Citrine will help you manifest prosperity every step of the way.

**Qualities:** Prosperity, abundance, success, manifestation, will.

**Good for:** Setting intentions, good luck.

**Issues:** Money issues, lack of self-belief.

**Mantra:** I am ready and open to receiving the blessings from the good intention I have set in my heart. I manifest prosperity in the pursuit of my soul dream.

# Decisiveness

## RUTILATED QUARTZ

Rutilated quartz takes you out of any stuffiness in your head or any division in your heart. It is a stone of a very fast vibration, so you can feel immediately alert. It quickens your mind, pulling you out of the sludge or chaos of indecision, and puts you in a lighter and clearer space to just commit. There is no wrong decision really, but the real question is what decision best serves my soul path? Rutilated quartz will help you meet that question with precision and grace.

Rutilated quartz is a very active stone, and one that accelerates your higher mind and the higher heart. The higher mind is a part of the spiritual energy body that is elevated from the fear-based convictions. The higher heart is part of the spiritual energy body that is elevated from the heart of your personal history, which may still carry hurts and pains of the past that are yet to be resolved on your path of evolution. Sometimes our hearts and minds can be clouded when it comes to judgement, but when the higher mind and higher heart are aligned and active, you can dispel fears and hurts and be clear and tuned in about what is right for you. Rutilated quartz takes you straight there, giving you fresh clarity and insight in order to be able to make the decisions that will best serve your soul path.

Decision-making is about commitment. When you commit to a decision with your total being, the rest of the universe will respond. Rutilated quartz amplifies the power of your commitment, making it a great ally for allowing the universe into your life to support with the manifestation of your intentions.

Rutilated quartz unifies your gut intuition with your spiritual faculties, to make decisions that will serve both your earthly and spiritual evolution. We will all get there eventually, whatever route we take, but there is a route that will be most nourishing in this instance. As a fast stone, rutilated quartz will align you with the life force to choose the path of least resistance. All you have to do is commit to your decision, and go for it. Work with the universe to allow the rest to unfold, trusting life without attachment to the outcome.

**Qualities:** Decisiveness.
**Good for:** Making important life changes.
**Issues:** Indecision, cloudy head.
**Mantra:** I commit to the decision that best serves my soul
  path!

A

# 7

# Air

*I am the divine seeker. I find peace, meaning, soulful purpose and connection with all that is.*

In the same way that all things are held in space, all the other elements are held in Air. Air represents our consciousness and consciousness is what holds all our experience. We expand our consciousness into deeper realms through the power of awareness. Starting with awareness of ourselves. The more we bring our conscious awareness to all parts of being the more alive and whole we become.

We are not the body, the emotions or the mind, we are the conscious awareness that contains and processes them all. Rather than become overly identified with our body, emotions and mind, and be unconsciously governed by them, we can bring the light of our conscious awareness to them, to process their signs and signals and expand and evolve.

The more we are unconsciously defined by our body, emotions and mind, the more contracted we become. The more we bring consciousness to the body, emotions and mind the more expanded we become.

All healing requires the power of our conscious awareness. To free ourselves from being prisoners of the fear-based self, we have to bring our conscious awareness to its tendencies and spiritualise it with our soul's truth.

Pain without spiritual consciousness is just pain. Pain with spiritual consciousness is our opportunity to change.

Conscious awareness is beautiful, because it is easy. It all starts with the simple act of just noticing. Without judgement or needing to control. Just noticing.

Scan your body. As the element of Air, what do you notice? Give what you notice the power of your attention, and ask what change it is asking for in your life.

Noticing is a journey that will uncover more and more of reality, until we feel expanded and connected in the divine nature of all that is. Our noticing will extend into the happy coincidences and synchronicities that enter our life as we become at one with the wholeness of the universe.

The shaman of the Air element is the divine seeker. She is an aspirant to serve the divine. She expands her awareness to connect with the wider symphony of the universe.

## AREA OF LIFE

Our Air element signifies our relationship with our inner spiritual life; the individual truth of our soul, our inner world and the richness that lies within it; dreams, imagination, longing. It is the place inside that only we know, and even parts that we don't yet know. It is the inner feeling and personal consciousness inside that we identify as 'I'; our dreaming self, our living self and our thinking self, inherently linked to our immortal true self. Like air, it is invisible and immaterial, we can't see it or touch it, but it is vital and it is what gives richness and meaning to our life. Air element is about the conscious relationship to our soul. The soul is who we are outside of time and space, innately part of the divine source of life and all that is. When the personal consciousness is in touch with the soul, then we feel whole. When we are out of touch with the soul we feel empty and that life is meaningless, and like we are just plodding along.

Like air, without soul, we don't breathe life into the body. We are not alive; we cannot reach any meaning. We feel empty inside, like zombies. Robotically moving through life, lacking in any real connection to ourselves or others. We lose faith in life. Our soul dream becomes unlived. A depression may even come over us to pull us inward, to ask us to stop and go deeper to reconnect with a deeper truth.

## SYMPTOMS OF AIR ELEMENT IMBALANCES

Weak Air occurs when a blockage and energy loss in our spiritual energy severs us from our spiritual relationship with our soul and its dream. Symptoms of an unlived soul life can lead to:

Depression
Lack of meaning and purpose
Addiction – to try and fill the void
Feeling lost and empty

Loneliness
Lack of trust
Spiritual crisis
Thinking too much/stuck in our heads

Excess Air occurs when we misuse our spiritual energy body or overidentify with the spiritual experience leading us to place our conscious awareness and ego disproportionately in other realms. It can lead to symptoms of:

Feeling spacey and ungrounded
Delusional or cut off from reality
Disconnected from the body
Displacement
Bypassing our emotional or psychological needs with a
    spiritual ego identity

## AIR ELEMENT IN OUR LIVES

**Energy body:** Spiritual energy body.

**Element qualities:** Faith, love, oneness, meaning, purpose.

**Areas of our life:** Our spiritual life.

**Relationships:** With our soul and the divine, something greater than ourselves.

**Chakras:** Crown (7th), Third Eye (6th), Heart (4th).

**Physical body areas:** Higher mind, heart.

**Energy body vitality needs:** Practices that nurture the space for our conscious awareness to be expanded, such as spiritual practices, prayer, meditation, yoga or working with crystals.

**Energy body vitality loss causes:** Broken hearts, losing faith, being too independent and not receiving help, suppressed soul life, being oppressed by society or relationships.

**Energy imbalance symptoms:**

*Underactive Air*: Depression, lack of meaning and purpose, addiction to try and fill the void, feeling lost and empty, overidentified with thoughts, thinking too much, stuck in our heads, robbing us of our psychic ability.

*Overactive Air*: Feeling spacey and ungrounded, delusional or cut off from reality, disconnected from the body, displacement.

## EXERCISE 12: CHECKING IN

Having read about Air element, check in with yourself and see what resonated for you. On a scale of one to ten, rate how fulfilled and balanced you feel in your Air element. Answer intuitively. If you don't know the answers, write about how you don't know the answers, bring your conscious awareness to not knowing, because the answers may just lie there. Reflect on questions such as:

How connected do you feel to your soul?
Do you feel meaning?
Are you being true to your soul?
Is your head congested with thoughts?

Note down your reflections here:

# EXERCISE 13: RECLAIMING VITALITY OF OUR SPIRITUAL ENERGY BODY

Where are we losing vitality and connection to our soul? These exercises allow us to identify factors that are at the root of an energy blockage or energy loss; so that we can then choose a crystal to help us reclaim that part of our self.

## EXERCISE 13A: VITALITY LOSS AND HEALING ORIGINAL WOUND

Did you recognise any spiritual energy vitality loss symptoms in your life? What might be the root causes of these symptoms? Use the descriptions in the 'energy body vitality loss causes' section of the box on page 201 to help you. Note down what resonates in the grid on the next page, write freely. Holistic healing seeks to address the root cause of the symptom, rather than the symptom itself, allowing for a true healing and trans- formation. Once you have identified causes in your life, choose a crystal from the Compass in the Air element that will support you to overcome these issues.

| ELEMENT | Energy blocks or energy loss symptoms and life patterns E.g. depression, lack of meaning and purpose, addiction to try and fill the void, feeling lost and empty, chatterbox mind robbing your power of awareness. | Causes E.g. broken hearts, losing faith, being too independent and not receiving help, suppressed soul life, oppressed individuality. |
| --- | --- | --- |
| AIR Spiritual energy body | | |

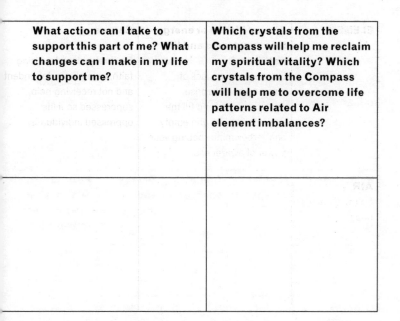

> What action can I take to support this part of me? What changes can I make in my life to support me?

> Which crystals from the Compass will help me reclaim my spiritual vitality? Which crystals from the Compass will help me to overcome life patterns related to Air element imbalances?

## EXERCISE 13B: RELATIONSHIP AUDIT

Assess your current spiritual relationships to see if they are meeting your soul needs and nurturing your connection to your soul and the divine. Spiritual relationships can be very empowering when we expand the power of our conscious awareness.

| Relationship | Nourishes energy? | Depletes energy? | Serves soul dream? | Fear-based self relationship or wholeness relationship? |
|---|---|---|---|---|
| A spiritual practice you have | | | | |
| A spiritual community you have | | | | |
| A spiritual teacher you have | | | | |
| Your soul and the divine God/ something greater than you | | | | |

In your current spiritual relationships, do they allow enough space for bringing in your awareness? If not, what can you do to balance this to meet your spiritual energy body's needs? What is your current relationship with your soul? And with the divine? Is it one of flow and connection? Or one of control? Is the nature of the relationship nourishing?

| Crystal insight meditation resolution: How can this relationship become more balanced? How might I reclaim myself both internally and externally? What actions do I need to take? | Which other crystals from the Compass might support you on your healing journey? |
| --- | --- |
| | |
| | |
| | |
| | |

## EXERCISE 13C:
## SPIRITUAL NOURISHMENT AUDIT

|  | **AUDIT** |
|---|---|
| **Self-nurturing and self-care** | How much do you nurture your spiritual energy body with conscious awareness? (1–10) |
| **Presence** | How present are you in your spiritual energy body? I.e. how much conscious awareness is available to you? (1–10) |

## CRYSTAL RESOLUTION

Reflect on the sources of nourishment such as spiritual practices that you enjoy etc. What can you do more of to nurture the vitality of your spiritual energy body? Which crystals can support you on that journey?

For overactive presence in the Air element use Earth crystals for grounding. For underactive Air presence use an Air crystal of your choice to enter a meditation practice that will bring a level of spiritual awareness into your life.

# Love

## ROSE QUARTZ

Rose quartz is one of the most important stones for mankind. It is a stone of the heart chakra and is best for spiritual healing.

The heart is the centre of the human experience. It can be hurt and retreat, or it can overflow in love and expand. One leads to separation and one leads to the realisation of oneness. This is the precarious nature of the human being's spiritual journey towards wholeness and truth.

It awakens the heart as the centre of our ability to love. That transcendent love which is the fabric of the universe, the source of all things and the love that connects us all. But also that human familial love, the love we share for those we care about the most. The love that can hurt but can also unite.

The heart is the centre for processing all of this. Rose quartz amplifies the heart's power to have compassion for ourselves and others. The hardest thing for us as human beings is when this capacity in us gets shut down.

Maybe a bad experience of pain, rejection or disappointment has caused our heart to close. Maybe we have been so hurt that we no longer feel safe to engage from that space. We may be reticent to give or receive from our heart, keeping it locked in a fearful cage. Whoever hurt you, maybe it is time to heal. To claim your heart back and relate again in the world in a way that will nourish your soul. Because love is the true language of the soul, it is the only thing that matters and the only thing that will take you home.

Whether it is a short or long road to healing, rose quartz will be an ally, amplifying your own compassionate wisdom to help you spiritually evolve from your pain. Rose quartz will help you mend your broken heart, it will help you heal and learn from the hurtful experience rather than be defined by it. It will open your heart space to enable you to move on.

One of our biggest wounds occurs when we fall out of love with ourselves. We treat ourselves badly, we inflict abuse on our bodies, and despise who we are.

More subtle forms of lack of self-love can be putting others' needs and opinions before the integrity of our soul, giving too much of ourselves, or allowing ourselves to be walked over by others. Self-love is key for any healing or spiritual development because ultimately you are love. Wearing rose quartz for long periods of time can be highly beneficial in restoring this loving relationship with yourself. You must put your heart first if you are to be of any true service to others.

Rose quartz raises your vibration, to love yourself, love others and love life.

**Qualities:** Love, compassion, self-love, healing.
**Good for:** Heart-centred spiritual awakening, mending
broken heart, healing relationships.
**Issues:** Heartbreak, self-hatred, lack of self-worth, rejection,
resentment.
**Mantra:** I am love.

# Magic

## LABRADORITE

Labradorite says, do you know how magic you are? Do you know your worth? Do you know that you are way more than the world says you are? Do you remember your magic powers?

Close your eyes. Listen to the silent hum of the universe that you are a part of. Awaken your heart to play in the magic of life. Abilities beyond your knowing are waiting to unfold if you listen.

Slip into the realm outside the immediate chatter in your head.

Listen to the universe singing in cosmic incantations, spells and energies, of dancing atoms in subtle communication and cooperation with each other. You can be in this space too. It is your space.

See past the veil of the fear-based self. You are a warrior of magic. Life is more than just the physical.

If your heart is pure, your magic will give you powers beyond your belief.

You will see through the veil and be able to read the energy behind all of life. Whether it be reading the planets, the stars, Tarot cards, omens in nature or any other method of divination, a labradorite stone will unlock your capacity to speak the language of the divine. Meditate with labradorite to find your language, find your magic tongue, find the dialect of your intuition. Chant in this language from your heart and hear the response from the magic energies of the universe, as all of life hears you.

Set intentions with labradorite, from your soul, like magic spells of goodness. Labradorite says 'Stir the cauldron of life. Move with the wind. Let life's mysteries move your bones. Be at one with it, to reveal that all is magic.'

Labradorite is the stone to work with to unleash your intuitive capacities, to manifest intentions with the help of the mysteries of life.

It will help you understand the coincidences and synchronicities to decipher your true path.

It will help you in working with energies that are your allies, that are steering you in the right direction all the time.

It will deepen you psychic abilities.

It will bring you into your power.

If you are a healer it will help you discern the energetic root cause of illnesses.

It will amplify your prayers and intentions.

It will amplify your intuition to discern whether or not somebody or something serves your soul dream, so you can get better with the choices you make.

It will help you read energy of other people or situations with tremendous precision so you can discern how to protect yourself. It will make you much more discerning about what energies you want to let into your world.

It will help you discern the major questions:

Will this person or situation deplete me of energy? Will this person or situation present an energy interference? Will this person or situation serve my soul dream? With labradorite by your side, your intuitive capabilities will be so on point that your intuition will give you a clear signal that repels you from anyone or any situation that doesn't serve your soul dream.

Labradorite will enhance your intuitive discernment even down to the smallest most mundane choices; for example, you'll be able to sense the energy behind the media you consume, the food and drink you choose, or the habits you have.

Try taking a piece of labradorite with you to the supermarket, see how it tunes you into the energy behind your choices. Your intuition may become more sensitive and you may feel repelled by certain foods, drinks, books, magazines, that are not serving your soul dream. It will help you discern what's going to steal your magic and what's going to awaken it.

Go spread your magic. Labradorite will help you access the multi-dimensionality of life and who you are.

**Qualities:** Magic, psychic seeing, psychic protection, discernment, intuition.

**Good for:** Enhancing psychic abilities, divination, entering into the spiritual/energetic healing arts, meditation, clairvoyance, working with energy, discerning who or what is an energy drain in your life.

**Issues:** Psychic blockages, spiritually disconnected.

**Mantra:** I am a goddess of magic.

# Psychic Clarity

## PURPLE FLUORITE

Purple fluorite brings clarity to your mind and your psychic centres.

It brings synthesis to conflicting energies in you that are interfering with your capacity to discern, and brings order, coherence and harmony to your energy field. Purple fluorite heals frequencies of dissonance and chaos, moving you from a state of confusion and fogginess to a state of clarity and insight.

Purple fluorite has a detoxifying effect on your pineal gland, the brain's link between the physical and spiritual realms. It cleanses the pineal gland of stagnant energies and interferences, almost immediately helping you to obtain a deep level of accuracy in your psychic and spiritual capacities.

Purple fluorite quickens and optimises the third eye chakra, restoring its true function to read emergent possibilities in your soul path and discern the best route for you. You can call it psychic vision, divination or seeing into the future. But really it is just accessing the reality outside of time and space, the dreaming world of everything that has ever been and everything there ever will be, reading the energy of options in the field of pure potentiality, and consciously choosing a route that will best serve your destiny.

This makes purple fluorite an excellent stone for decision-making, and becoming very mentally clear about what it is you want and what goals will most serve your soul dream. If you are unclear and caught between options or ideas of what you could do, purple fluorite is good to have on hand. Spend a few moments of quiet meditation with purple fluorite, closing your eyes, working through the options, asking what would my life be like if I chose this route? Not with neediness, desperation or attachment, but with openness. Trust the psychic power of what comes up.

Purple fluorite is the stone for mental clarity. Have it on hand for any tasks that require attention to detail or the ordering of complex information. This makes it great for writing, editing, planning or any tasks that involve processing large amounts of information.

If you are feeling overwhelmed and confused with thoughts or ideas, purple fluorite is a wonderful stone for organising your thoughts, and synthesising different ideas into workable solutions.

Fluorite comes in many colours – green, pink, golden, black. They all have the same specialism in that they bring harmony and order to the spiritual and psychic centres, but the different colours will be imbued with their own qualities.

Pink and green are great for bringing order and clarity in the spiritual capacities of the heart. Golden will clear your solar plexus and help your mind get focused with your direction and purpose. Black works in a similar way black tourmaline in that it cleanses you of any energetic interferences or false self-narratives that may be hanging on.

**Qualities:** Mental clarity, psychic clarity, order, harmony.

**Good for:** Clearing energy field, problem-solving, decision-making, editing, processing lots of information.

**Issues:** Confused, overwhelmed, poor concentration.

**Mantra:** I am clear, I think clearly, I see clearly, I perceive clearly and I make my decision.

# Spiritual Healing

## AMETHYST

The queen of crystals, amethyst aligns all your chakras and balances your elements, empowering you to take your place in life, remembering your divine nature.

Amethyst is a stone of regal solitude. Sometimes we need to sit alone, meditatively to reconnect with ourselves and our divine essence. Meditating with amethyst can deepen our meditative states and conjure up feelings, images or symbols that are significant to our spiritual growth.

Amethyst is also a stone of purification, warding off negative influences. She works all the way through each chakra, working her magic, in fluttering motions, cleansing away anything that is clinging on and disturbing our divine connection.

In our search for meaning and connection, we can often take on habits or addictions in an attempt to fill the void. These habits and addictions can become energetic entities in us with lives of their own, emitting their own energy signatures, dulling our connection with our divinity and soul. Addictions have a birth, an original wound that they are feeding off. Amethyst energetically works at healing the original wound, killing off the energy source of the addiction, and restoring your connection to your divine glow. Sleeping with amethyst under your pillow, or having amethyst in your bedroom, will loosen the stronghold of the entities that keep you in addiction, and support you on your healing journey to freedom.

At moments where you are most triggered to engage in addictive behaviours, amethyst will help you name the entity, and its needs, without succumbing to it. Keep asking yourself, who is winning? The entity or your sovereignty? Amethyst is your cheerleader for team sovereignty.

Amethyst raises your vibration to one of regal and divine power, enabling you to embody more of your soul dream, to ward off these influences.

Amethyst is a great stone to have to set up a meditative sacred space in your home, such as an altar or shrine.

Amethyst is also great at cleansing other crystals. Place your other crystals on an amethyst bed, to draw out any lower energies they have absorbed.

Amethyst can be of good use for those who are experiencing a spiritual crisis, such as the 'dark night of the soul' or an existential crisis. Amethyst moves you towards spiritual realisation and healing.

**Qualities:** Divine connection, purification, protection.

**Good for:** Deepening spiritual journey, meditation, creating a sacred space, protecting your home from negative influences, healing addictive behaviours that are interfering with soul dream.

**Issues:** Addictions, habits, spiritual crisis.

**Mantra:** I remember my divine nature and know my worth. I purify myself of influences interfering with my connection.

# Spiritual Awareness

## APOPHYLLITE

Hold on to an apophyllite in meditation and taste the frequency of your original light. Let it elevate you to transpersonal dimensions of the higher self, and expand your awareness.

In spiritual work apophyllite can be your greatest ally. It awakens you to the spiritual nature of all things, and the transcendent spiritual reality outside of time and space. Meditating with apophyllite can help you reach very pure transcendent states and help you gain spiritual insight or spiritual guidance that will serve your development.

If you are struggling with overcoming an issue in the lower energy bodies such as an issue around vitality, emotion, or power, meditating with apophyllite can give you a higher perspective and give you the spiritual insight you need to resolve that issue and spiritually evolve from it. Apophyllite is a master stone at connecting you to the spiritual guidance of your soul dream.

Apophyllite is a purifying stone and clears the energetic channels that connect you with the divine. Whereas other purifying crystals such as black tourmaline and obsidian work on purifying the dimensions of the physical, emotional and mental body, apophyllite works on clearing the astral and celestial layers of your spiritual energy body, which are your bridge between your material body and higher realities.

Purification at this level restores your faith and connection to spirit in a very clear and profound way, and has the effect of bridging communication with angelic realms and spiritual guides. Apophyllite has similar properties to selenite in this sense, but whereas selenite's energy is soft, supportive and blissful, apophyllite gives you more of a mental and direct experience of ascension. Its ability to expand the mental faculties to transcendent states makes it a perfect stone for meditation.

If you are going to engage in spiritual work, such as inner work, or spiritual healing, spending some time with apophyllite can prepare you, getting you in the right space to get the most spiritual insight out of your experience.

Green apophyllite has the same effect as clear or white apophyllite except it connects you more to nature spirits and the spiritual realms of Mother Earth.

**Qualities:** Spiritual awareness, spiritual growth and evolution, spiritual insight.

**Good for:** Meditating, raising spiritual vibration of spaces, preparation for spiritual healing.

**Issues:** Lack of faith and connection.

**Mantra:** I am elevated in the realms of ascension and choose the healing path of my highest spiritual evolution.

# Self-knowledge

## LAPIS LAZULI

Lapis lazuli is a stone of inner discovery and spiritual growth. It is a stone that was used widely by ancient civilisations such as the Ancient Egyptians.

Lapis lazuli is quite a serious stone. It takes you into another dimension of yourself. It gives you almost a position of regality, as it elevates you to state of consciousness where you can become a sacred witness to your inner life, and a master of your kingdom. Lapis lazuli gives you the psychic vision to see unconscious patterns and negative influences in your life, and reclaim your power from them.

Lapis lazuli pulls you inward and shifts you into a quiet state of awareness where you can enter deep meditative contemplation in which you may encounter inner visions or sensations that reveal something about yourself.

Lapis lazuli is a great stone to use if you are engaging in inner work, and are seeking to evolve past issues or patterns that you want to let go of. Meditating with lapis lazuli to contemplate issues will allow you to enter a higher wisdom and gain deeper spiritual insight into the situation. Lapis lazuli brings you into a realm of consciousness where negative thoughts do not influence you, giving you an elevated perspective and a deep sense of peace.

If you are involved in a situation that you want to rise above, lapis lazuli will give you a sense of composure and non-attachment so that you can act with grace and divine wisdom. But lapis lazuli won't let you get away with assuming the spiritual high ground, it will always reveal the role that your karmic patterns or unconscious attitudes have played, so that you can take the responsibility to evolve from them.

Lapis lazuli is the ultimate stone for spiritual development, psychic insight and reflection. All these things come from knowing yourself first. The journey of spiritual evolution always begins with you.

**Qualities:** Self-knowledge, spiritual development, psychic insight, sovereignty, evolution.

**Good for:** Inner work, meditation, life reflection, uncovering your truth.

**Issues:** Negative habits and life patterns.

**Mantra:** I rise from the drama and attachments and see the truth of my being.

# Faith

## SELENITE

A celestial stone, selenite can make you feel floaty, blissful and imbued with divine love. It unlocks the purity in you and unlocks your softer side.

If you have been highly critical and particularly harsh on yourself or on someone else, selenite can soften the harsh inner critic in you, and show you it's time to be a little more gentle and loving on yourself and others.

If you are someone who ordinarily rejects intimacy and connection, selenite will have you feeling so light and fluffy that you won't be able to help being gentle with someone who needs it.

Sometimes life can harden us in a conviction that we have to take care of everything ourselves. We can become so fiercely independent that we shut down our crown chakra and block our capacity to receive heavenly support. Selenite will soften this hardness in your energy field and uplift you in the reassurance that you are not alone and are loved and supported by higher planes of existence.

This makes selenite the better-known crystal for communing with spiritual guides or angelic beings. Do not expect angels descending from the heavens into your living room in all their glory, telling you your destiny. The language of the ethereal realms is gentle and non-linear. You can find the guidance in your heart. Notice the quality of feelings that are being transmitted in your experience with selenite. Or the symbols or visions that arise in your meditation. The intelligence of your light body will be activated for you to integrate this guidance in a way beyond words.

Selenite will help you develop this transcendent relationship with your light being and other light beings. If you are feeling blocked in accessing guidance from these transcendent inner landscapes, selenite will support you.

Having selenite in key points in your home can raise the vibration of your space and invite in loving energies.

**Qualities:** Faith, spiritual guidance, light body activation, spiritual bliss.

**Good for:** Receiving help, asking the angelic realms for help or guidance.

**Issues:** Serious, hardened by life, feeling alone, critical, rejecting intimacy and connection.

**Mantra:** I awaken to the frequency of light and love and receive guidance from these realms. I have faith in life. I am supported from above and I am not alone.

# Insight

## SODALITE

Sodalite heightens the capacity of the throat chakra. The throat chakra isn't only the centre of your voice and how you communicate in the world, it is also the centre through which the universe communicates to you.

It is through the throat chakra that we are in subtle relationship with the humming, dancing atoms that make up all of life. Everything in the universe is essentially an aggregation of vibrating atoms. The collective silent hum of all vibrating matter could be called the voice of the universe, or rather the symphony or orchestra of the whole. Each thing in the universe is vibrating at a different rate or frequency depending on its unique quality. We are emitting a vibration all the time, through which we transmit what is going on in our energy bodies at any given time.

If something or someone's vibration doesn't resonate with your own frequency, it is through the throat chakra that we read this dissonance and have a sensation that something is off or not right for us. It is through the throat chakra that this information gets transmitted and we get a sense of the vibration of energy in the air.

Sodalite has the ability to clear the back of the throat chakra, which is often quite guarded or not yet awakened. This opening strengthens our capacity to read the energy of an environment or a person, so that we gain added insight about a situation. If the hum doesn't feel right, you can trust what is being transmitted and name it, so that you bring it into consciousness for yourself.

If you have to make a decision regarding something that you are unclear about, holding sodalite can be useful. It can add the dimension of reading the vibration of the options you have, giving you additional insight into whether or not the choice resonates with the core of your being. Sometimes our fears can interrupt this natural process, and we can make decisions that resonate most with the safety of our fears, or with the naivety of our fantasies or desires. Sodalite clears some of this interference so we can get in touch with the frequency of the soul dream, and measure energy against that instead of against our fears or fantasies.

When we are asking, 'Do I want to allow this energy in to my life?' sodalite can be a good companion.

Sodalite also activates the third eye. It communicates the vibrational material from the throat chakra to the third eye, and strengthens the thirds eye's capacity to understand the nature of that material and what it means on your soul path. This makes it great for deepening your divination abilities, such as reading Tarot, reading omens from the universe, I Ching or any other system you have for breaking down the energy of patterns to see where they may lead.

As the language of vibration and energy is subtle, so too is sodalite a subtle stone. But the results can be powerful when you strengthen this intuitive dimension of yourself.

**Qualities:** Insight, divination.

**Good for:** Reading energy, decision-making, deepening wisdom, soul path guidance.

**Issues:** Indecision, overcoming naivety.

**Mantra:** I awaken to the silent hum of the universe and read the energy of the world with accuracy and fluidity, to help give me insight into my soul path.

# Divine Purpose

## OPTICAL CALCITE

Optical calcite is like the order after chaos, or the calm after the storm. It gives you the space for enlightened composure and reflection after being in the throes of emotion.

The different varieties have their own nuances, but the core quality of optical calcite is its ability to elevate your seeing to bring order and clarity.

Optical calcite raises your head above the drama and attachments in life, to give you the insight to know the right next move which will be a win for your soul.

Order and chaos is like a divine formula for the growth and expression of the universe. In creation, we see patterns of harmony and order that are born from the seemingly random and unpredictable. Optical calcite is aligned to the divine principle that helps give birth to order.

This makes it great for things like editing, organising information or finding clarity in confusion. It's a stone of refinement.

All situations, however chaotic, have a divine purpose, and can eventually support you in finding your divine purpose. But this requires you to reach an elevated place of seeing, where you are not attached to your personal history and story.

Optical calcite is like the liminal meeting point between the true self and the fear-based self, the place where your divine purpose is becoming clear. Optical calcite will help you see and take action from this place, whether it be in a relationship, your career, a creative project or any significant issue that is causing turbulence and confusion about your life path.

Optical calcite tames wildness and lifts the haze of the fears that keep you from your divine purpose. It realigns your gaze to get serious and fix your true eyes on the true prize. Instead of getting stuck in repetitive patterns or attachments, optical calcite will help you to learn the true lessons that will serve your evolution, so that you can move forward in your divine purpose. It may be that you need to forgive and let go, or remedy a situation – whatever the soul lesson is, optical calcite will help you see it. This makes optical calcite an equally good stone as the quartz to use as a soul dream diagnostic tool, to discern between the one-sidedness of your fears and the wisdom of the soul dream.

Optical calcite helps you get clear in your intention.

Everything in your life is driven by your intention. Whether it be conscious or unconscious, your intentions influence what you create and manifest in life. Optical calcite helps you see from a higher ground any unconscious intentions that have been fear-based that are keeping you stuck in your life. Optical calcite aligns you to higher intentions that will serve your highest potential and help you to manifest the truth of your soul dream.

All varieties of optical calcite hold these qualities, but use your intuition to see which varieties you are drawn to, as each variety will imbue any additional qualities that you might require at that time. Trust your intuition to choose.

**Qualities:** Divine purpose, moving forward, order, clarity, neutrality, determination.

**Good for:** Self-reflection, finding your soul path, seeing clearly in drama, editing or refining creative projects, organising, decluttering, discerning soul dream wisdom.

**Issues:** Chaotic life, feeling lost and confused, overactive emotions, lacking direction, repetitive life patterns.

**Mantra:** I see the divine order in the chaos and move forward with divine purpose.

# Communication

## BLUE LACE AGATE

Blue lace agate channels a great light and opening through the throat chakra, bringing order and clarity to what it is you need to express from your soul.

Blue lace agate emanates a gentle confidence in what is true for you, giving you the eloquence, grace and fluidity to speak your ideas into reality. Words carry power, but only if there is energy behind them. Sometimes the power of the voice can be squashed by inhibition, lack of confidence or imbalanced power dynamics in relationships, which make it difficult for us to be heard.

Blue lace agate is a great stone for removing old blockages and restoring energy to your throat chakra, helping you to believe in yourself and transmit power in what it is you need to communicate. It is great for difficult conversations, where you need to find the right words to speak from your heart.

If you are shy in communicating with others or if you experience social anxiety in situations where you need to speak up and shine, blue lace agate can be a great ally to keep in your pocket, to help you feel safe and carefree so that you can be yourself. It is great for all kinds of public speaking or work that is dependent on the strength of your communication skills, such as jobs involving big presentations or pitches. It can also be of assistance in writing or articulating difficult concepts.

Blue lace agate has a very calming effect on the voice, which can be of assistance to those who need to slow down or reduce the intensity of how they speak.

It is a slower-vibration stone so is of most benefit when used over longer periods of time, making it a great stone for jewellery that you can wear often or tumbled stones that you can keep in your pockets and have with you throughout the day.

**Qualities:** Communication, clarity, eloquence.

**Good for:** Public speaking, writing, articulating difficult ideas, speaking your truth, being heard.

**Issues:** Social anxiety, lack of confidence in communication, speech difficulties.

**Mantra:** I speak from my heart with fluidity and grace.

# 8

# The Cure-All

## CLEAR QUARTZ

Clear Quartz. Or King Quartz as I like to call it. The clear quartz crystal is not in the Compass as it is a bit of an all-element, all-chakra, all-singing, all-dancing, cure-all stone. If you only had to get one crystal, get a clear quartz. Clear quartz acts like a reiki healer in that it channels life force energy to do its work on you. And life force knows best. Clear quartz amplifies life force energy in you to correct your energy distribution and flow in the places you most need it.

Quartz is an all-round balancing and cleansing stone. It is a stone of clarity, so is great to use when you feel congested or confused about something, or you feel like you just need a good clearing-out in your energy field. Clear quartz can absorb energies for you and transmute them into neutral energy. But as a stone that absorbs energy it is best that you regularly cleanse your clear quartz crystals.

You can also programme a clear quartz to a specific use, just with the power of your intention. To programme a quartz for a specific use, simply cleanse the stone first then hold it, and either inwardly or out loud, with every fibre of your being, state your intention of what you wish the stone to be used for, letting the quartz know that you are available and ready to receive or express what you want to bring into your life. The quartz will amplify the intention and work with life force to influence the rest of the universe to respond to that intention.

Quartz can also be programmed to use as a tool. For example, in the exercise on page 61 [Exercise 5] I recommend programming a quartz as a diagnostic tool, to help you with unlocking the wisdom in your tension. You could even programme a quartz to replicate the quality of another stone. It may not be as effective but is always good as an interim measure.

Placing quartz crystals in the corners of your home, programming them to absorb any rogue energies in the place, is very effective, especially if you have been feeling as though the energy of your space is slightly off. Again, be sure to cleanse your quartz as often as you remember. Cleansing in water will do.

I recommend everyone have a quartz!

**Qualities:** Clarity, amplifying, cleansing, absorbing, cure-all.
**Good for:** Everything!
**Issues:** Anything!
**Mantra:** I am fresh, clean and all things new and improved. I amplify my qualities and abilities in life. I cleanse myself of anything incongruent to that.

# Conclusion

Life is magic. Especially when we let magic into our lives.

We can find ourselves in versions of who we think we ought to be. But we really find our self when we allow the power of our soul to express itself through the joys and challenges of life's ups and downs. We find wholeness, and we become part of the whole, and can enjoy the ride of cooperating with the universe as she gives us happy coincidences and synchronicities to help us on our way.

Crystals are a proof of magic, and I hope through this book they will provide a little sparkle in your life, in your journey of self-discovery and reconnecting with the divinity that is you and the universe.

Everything starts with relationship. Relationship with the body and the earth, relationship with ourselves and each other, relationship with our power and soul path, and our relationship with something greater than us, of which we are all a unique expression.

In your unique expression, there are many parts of you; the divine seeker of the Air element, the warrior of the Fire element, the intuitive tracker of the Water element and the ally of the earth of the Earth element. There are many qualities and strengths waiting to come forth in all elements as we meet with life.

Sometimes we may be shy or scared to bring all parts of ourselves out, or unconsciously restrict our self through old learnt habits and behaviours. But when life commands us to bring forth who we are, we will know by the signs and symptoms we experience as tension. Tension is a sign that life force is working its way through our door, to push us in the direction of our path and help us give birth to our soul dream. The only reason it is uncomfortable is because of our resistance to the unknown.

And if the tension gets overwhelming or hard to figure out or get through, crystals can be our best friends and our guides. They amplify what we really are, beneath the suffering of what we are not.

Across each element we can reclaim all aspects of what we may have lost or what we are trying to find. All parts of the divine seeker, the warrior, the tracker and the ally of the earth are waiting to be expressed in us, to find a life of wholeness and harmony and, more importantly, magic.

Because when we touch our magic, all of life – even the tough parts – can be a little bit special.

Protect your magic. Protect your beautiful energy bodies and trust what they are telling you.

By the power of Earth, nourish your physical body and manifest firm foundations to survive and thrive.

By the power of Water, work with rather than against your emotions to unlock your wisdom and intuitive power. Let Water guide you on your path of least resistance.

By the power of Fire, go out there and manifest your soul dream! Light up the world with your creativity, individuality and unique service to the world.

By the power of Air, bring the light of your awareness to the wholeness of your soul and the oneness of all there is.

Crystals – these little beauties of harmony and balance – will change your energy signature for each element whenever you are feeling out of whack in your journey to finding your own harmony.

We can do what we can to bring our awareness towards parts of our soul that are seeking to come through to bring about healing, resolution and growth in our life. But it is not always easy when life demands get in the way, and we can forget to check in with our self. It is only when the tension in our energy bodies gets loud enough that we have to finally make change. Crystals can be your safe space to check in with yourself and help you to be the change, embody the change and express the change in everything you do. They are a perfect embodiment of balance in their quality; all they can do is teach us through correcting our frequency. The rest lies with our awareness and intention to make the difference.

We are divine and have all the answers, crystals just help us to amplify our divinity so that we can reveal our true self. And the world needs more true selves.

Be kind to yourself and above all listen to the intelligence of your being; it seeks to reveal the depth of your soul and guide you on your path. Trust what is coming up for you physically, emotionally, mentally and spiritually, and seek to get to the root cause of the tension you are feeling so that you make meaningful leaps and bounds towards finding your truth.

Protect your energy bodies and the energy that you bring into your life, so that you can find your balance and spread your joy.

And you too can emanate the harmony in your energy field. Just like a crystal.

## EXPLORING OTHER STONES

*The Crystal Compass* explores 40 of the most accessible and abundantly available stones, that can change your world. If you are interested in rarer stones, you can research Synergy 12 stones, which are a rarer set of high vibrational stones. The world is abundant with different types of crystals. I chose these 40, (41 if you include good old King Clear Quartz) for their power, ability, strength, good value in terms of price, and availability. I find these 40 the most useful stones but there are many to explore if it takes your interest.

# Symptoms Index

Addiction, 104, 218
Anger, 156
Anxiety, 85, 101, 140, 145, 147, 181

Bad mood, 137, 143, 150
Blood health, 85
Bullying, 189

Career issues, 101
Confused, 215, 229
Congested, 104
Control freak, 147

Decisiveness, 194, 215, 226
Depression, 140, 143
Doubt, 130, 181

Emotional imbalance, 140, 145, 156, 229
Energy body loss, 85, 140
Exhaustion, 88

Family issues, patterns, 107
Financial issues, 103, 192
Forgetfulness, 88
Forgiveness, 153
Frustration, 130, 145

Grief, 143, 147

Heartbreak, 143, 210
Home or housing issues, 101
Hungover, 82

Intuition, 130

Laziness, 82
Life patterns, 107, 222, 229
Lost, 229
Low confidence or self-esteem, 135, 176, 181, 189, 210

Memory loss, 130
Menstrual cycle, 130

Negative energy, 93, 104, 137
Negative thinking, 137, 147

Overthinking, 137
Overwhelm, 140, 215

Panic attacks, 85
Passion, 184
Phobias, 137
Post-traumatic stress, 118, 120, 141
Premature ageing, 88
Procrastination, 82, 176, 181

Rejection, 210
Relationship issues, 147
Resentment, 153, 210

Sadness, 143, 156, 147
Shock, 85, 140
Shyness, 176, 181, 187, 189
Sluggishness, 82
Spinal health and posture, 85
Spiritual crisis, 218
Stress, 88, 99, 104
Stuck, 143
Suppressed emotions, 150

Tense muscles, 82, 99
Toxic environments, 93, 104
Toxic relationships, 93, 104, 187
Trauma, 85, 140, 156

Work-life balance, 90
Worry, 99, 137

# Results Index

Abundance, 90, 192
Acceptance, 147
Action, 82, 176
Ancestral healing, 109
Assertiveness, 181, 184, 189

Balance, 101, 145

Calming, 140
Centring, 101, 140
Clarity, 181, 215, 229, 232, 235
Cleansing, 93, 104, 235
Comforting, 140, 143
Communication, 150, 232
Compassion, 145, 153, 210
Concentration, 82, 215
Confidence, 176, 181, 189
Courage, 109
Creativity, 130, 134, 176, 179, 184

Determination, 97, 229
Detoxing, 85, 93, 104
Discipline, 97
Divine Feminine, 130, 134
Divine Purpose, 229
Dreams (understanding
   dreams), 130

Ecstasy, 137
Efficiency, 82
Energising, 82, 136
Expression, 134, 150, 181, 232

Faith, 147, 220, 224
Fertility, 88, 143

Goal-setting (heart-centred),
   145
Gratitude, 137
Grounding, 82, 85, 93, 140

Harmony, 137, 215
Healing, 156, 210, 218
Health, 90
Hope, 147

Innovation, 181
Insight, 226
Inspiration, 134, 184
Intuition, 134, 212
Invigorating, 88

Joy, 137, 176

Leadership, 186
Letting go, 147, 153, 156
Love, 210

Magic, 212
Memory, 88
Motivation, 97, 184

Nature (connecting with), 89
New beginnings, 88

Oneness, 153
Optimism, 148

Patience, 130
Peace, 137
Perseverance, 97
Power, 134, 145, 187, 189
Practicality, 85
Pregnancy, 88
Presence, 85
Problem-solving, 143, 181, 215
Prosperity, 192
Protection, 93, 104, 189, 212, 218
Psychic ability, 212, 215, 226
Purification, 104, 218

Rationality, 101
Refreshing, 82
Rejuvenation, 88
Relaxing, 99
Renewal, 88
Revitalising, 88, 176

Security, 101
Self-awareness, 150
Self-care, 99
Self-knowledge, 130, 222, 226
Serenity, 147
Sexuality, 176, 179, 184
Soothing, 140

Spiritual awareness, or development 218, 220, 222
Spiritual guidance, 224, 226
Spontaneity, 88
Stability, 101, 145
Strength, 82, 97, 107, 189
Success 181, 192

Truth, 150, 222

Unwinding, 100
Uplifting, 143

Willpower, 82, 97
Wisdom, 130, 226

Youthfulness, 88

# Acknowledgements

Thanks are due to all who helped in the process of this book. To my mum, my life-giver, my inspiration, my everything, to whom I am indebted, thank you for all you have ever done and for your daily words of encouragement while I was writing. I love you. To Stanya, thank you for helping me find my voice, in the storm of my edge; working with you has been life-affirming and life-changing. To my darling bear, thank you for your love, patience, support, bear wisdom and for the gift of being able to grow together during the gruelling few months of writing!!! I love you. To Anuka, across time and space always a soul sister, I am so lucky and blessed that it is so, thank you for your truth, wisdom and friendship; you are my way-shower. To Daniel and everyone at the Mac Rental Company, thank you for saving my life on numerous occasions with your amazing service. Thank you to Elif of www.elifc.net, for your lovely illustrations.

To all the teachers and mentors on my path who I have been blessed to work with and without whom this book would not be possible. There are many, but a particular mention to those who have been especially influential in this book; Arnold Mindell, whose work on the dreambody continues to inspire me deeply; Lisa Morgan, from Green Island, Jamaica to Green Lane,

Ulverston, I am so grateful our family lives have been inter-twined and for what I have learned from you, as teacher and as honorary Auntie!!; Nathaniel Hughes, for your heart-centred work, it really enlivened my world with spirit and transformed my relationship with shamanism at a pivotal time while writing. And to anyone who has been a client of mine, thank you for the privilege of sharing your soul journey with me, you have been my greatest teachers, I love you.

To my family, my inspiration; my siblings Adenike, Zac and Zico, and my Dad for always believing in us; to my Grandad for your integrity and for guiding us by your example and your amazing life stories; to my other grandparents and ancestors who are beyond the veil, I give thanks for your life, we are who we are because of you. To Steve, you live on in the kind gestures and things you did for others, you are in our hearts and I remember you as I work from the desk you made.

To my incredible friends for your amazing support; to Emma, Alice and Nell for always providing a space for authenticity, love, growth and adventure, and my life-long friends Boo, Sima and Azadeh, for the blessing of love and longevity in friendship. Thank you to Zulma for your teaching, Eugenia for your holding and all the sisters for your love.

A massive thank you to Olivia Morris at Orion Publishing, for trusting me with this project and for all your encouragement along the way, and a heartfelt thanks to the rest of the Orion team.

# About the Author

Aisha Amarfio is a shamanic healer and energy medicine practitioner, with a busy clinic in London. After training as a Reiki Master, Clinical Hypnotherapist and Master NLP Practitioner, she embarked on a five-year journey of training in the shamanic healing arts. Aisha's work has been commonly described as life-changing. She has helped hundreds of clients to overcome chronic issues or blockages, to experience spiritual self-discovery, transformation, and inspired creativity from the heart.

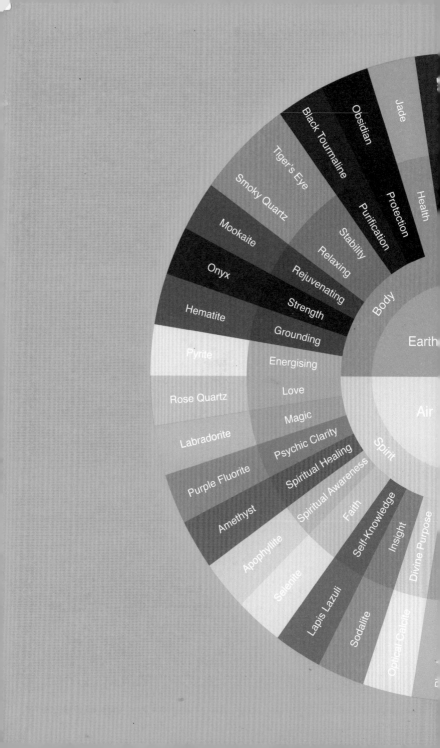